Step-by-Step
OUTDOOR
BRICKWORK

Step-by-Step
OUTDOOR
BRICKWORK

Over twenty easy-to-build projects
for your yard and garden

Penny Swift and Janek Szymanowski

AURA BOOKS

NEW
HOLLAND

First published in the UK in 1992 by
New Holland (Publishers) Ltd
37 Connaught Street, London W2 2AZ

ISBN 1 85368 090 7 (hbk)
ISBN 1 85368 091 5 (pbk)

Consultant Editors: David Holloway, Mike Lawrence
Editor: Elizabeth Rowe
Designer: Phil Gorton
Cover designer: Phil Gorton
Illustrators: Tom Cross, Bruce Snaddon
Phototypeset by Tradespools Ltd, Somerset
Originated by Daylight Colour Art Pte Ltd, Singapore
Printed and bound in Singapore by Kyodo Printing Co. Pte Ltd

CONTENTS

INTRODUCTION

THIS BOOK IS ABOUT USING MASONRY IN THE GARDEN OR BACKYARD. BY MASONRY, WE MEAN BRICKS AND BLOCKS, CONCRETE AND STONE, GRAVEL AND SAND AND THE VARIOUS PRODUCTS MADE WITH THEM. THE GARDEN OR BACKYARD IS IDEALLY AN EXTENSION OF THE HOUSE AND AS SUCH SHOULD REFLECT YOUR LIFESTYLE AND CATER TO YOUR OUTDOOR NEEDS. THE FEATURES YOU INCORPORATE AND THE WAY IN WHICH THEY ARE BUILT WILL GIVE YOUR SITE ITS PARTICULAR CHARACTER AND STYLE. WHETHER YOU ARE INTRODUCING A TRICKLING WATER FEATURE, LAYING A PATIO OR BUILDING A WALL, THE MATERIALS USED, NATURAL OR MAN-MADE, SHOULD WHEREVER POSSIBLE REFLECT THE MATERIALS OF THE HOUSE OR THE MATERIALS USED IN OTHER OUTDOOR FEATURES.

In the book we will look at a comprehensive range of masonry jobs you can do outside. We will be covering pools and ponds (including accessories for creating fountains and waterfalls and for lighting); brick-built planters; outdoor furniture and barbecues; steps in various materials; pillars and arches; patios; paths and drives; walls (including retaining walls and concrete screen block walling); and, finally, the construction of a concrete panel garage.

Each section has step-by-step drawings or photographs showing how the job is done and details of tools, materials and masonry techniques are given in the reference section starting on page 80.

SOME BASIC RULES

Good planning is essential when it comes to outside masonry work. Consider carefully the existing character of the site and your house before you start to plan any additional structures. For certain projects you may also need to consult the local planning authority.

Decide what you want, where you want it and then choose the materials which will provide the best appearance and function.

Scale drawings will help enormously when planning the work – it's better to make your mistakes on paper rather than on the ground when undoing them later can be difficult, if not impossible.

Think about levels, existing fixed structures, services (especially underground pipes and cables), slopes, and finally soil type (all masonry work is more difficult on soft or clay soils).

Good workmanship and the use of quality materials are important if your structures are to be a sound investment. Remember that well-planned garden masonry work will add to the value of your house when it is time to sell.

Above right: *Bricks and concrete used in a planter, patio and steps.*

Far right: *Reconstituted stone edging used as both a border and a coping.*

Right: *An effective, sinuous brick path.*

Below: *A seat built between planters.*

PLANTERS

RAISED FLOWER BEDS AND PLANTERS BUILT IN OR ONTO WALLS CAN ADD TO THE VISUAL IMPACT OF MOST OUTDOOR AREAS, PROVIDING COLOUR AND FORM. THEY ARE EASIER TO MAINTAIN AND REQUIRE LESS WATERING THAN POTS AND FREE-STANDING CONTAINERS. PLANTERS ARE PARTICULARLY USEFUL FOR SITES WITH POOR SOIL, AS YOU CAN FILL THEM WITH ANY GOOD QUALITY SOIL MIX YOU WANT. WHATEVER KIND OF PLANT CONTAINER YOU DECIDE TO BUILD, THE BASIC PRINCIPLES REMAIN THE SAME.

FUNCTION

Raised planters are usually built against walls, as part of retaining walls or as features arising from existing paving – most typically to frame the entrance to a home. Being raised off the ground, their leafy contents can effectively soften the hard lines of an adjoining wall, or add interest to a dull area.

A practical reason for building a raised planter would be to make a low-lying, swampy area suitable for planting. Vegetables are often grown in this way when drainage is a problem. A raised planter is also a boon to gardeners who are elderly or disabled, since, built to a suitable height, it eliminates the need for bending. Whole gardens can be created with raised flower beds especially for wheelchair users.

Building a raised planter on a patio or as part of a pool surround can successfully enclose and define the area. Planted with pretty flowers, it will add colour; with foliage plants or shrubs, it creates a feeling of privacy.

In a level setting lacking interesting features, the addition of raised beds can create varying levels, improving the landscape and providing character. Use them to frame colourful plants, to break up a large expanse of lawn, or in the place of a dividing wall within the confines of your property.

A free-standing planter constructed alongside built-in seating may become the dominant feature on a patio, adding a decorative touch. If planted with a colourful and striking species, it can have a dramatic effect, as in the planter built in our step-by-step project.

DRAINAGE

A big advantage of raised planters is that they can simply be left open at the base, thus enclosing the plants but allowing for good drainage. However, weepholes should also be included in the design to ensure that the roots do not become waterlogged. See retaining walls, page 68 for details of how to create weepholes and ensure proper drainage.

Additional drainage is especially important when constructing a planter next to the walls of a house. In this case, the inclusion of damp proofing is also essential to prevent moisture from entering the house. This may be in the form of black plastic secured against the back wall of the planter; otherwise a suitable bitumen (asphalt tar) sealant may be painted on the area.

MATERIALS

Planters are commonly built with bricks which are durable and easy to maintain. Facing brick will look especially good if it has been used elsewhere in the garden while clay bricks or inexpensive cement bricks may be used and then rendered (pargeted) and painted. Concrete block walling can be used in place of brick, especially if it blends with other wall or paving features.

Successful raised planters may be constructed from hardwood – the most suitable being railway sleepers (railroad ties) or wooden poles. However, the wood must be treated with preservative and thoroughly sealed, otherwise it will rot over time. A raised bed of unmortared bricks could also be built and can easily be shifted or removed should you decide to alter the layout of your garden or backyard at a later stage.

A mixture of materials is sometimes very effective – for instance, a brick planter with a tiled or wooden coping adds texture and variety to the site. Whatever material you choose, though, make sure it blends harmoniously with the house and the other outdoor features.

Step-by-step planter

To build a planter 800 x 700 mm (2 ft 7 in x 2 ft 3 in) and with a height of 490 mm (19 in) from the foundation and 380 mm (15 in) from the paving, and with a foundation 1,000 × 900 mm (3 ft 3 in × 3 ft) and 100 mm (4 in) deep, you will need:

Foundation
25 kg (or just over ½ x 100 lb bag) cement
65 kg or 1¾ cu ft (143 lb) sand
100 kg or 2 cu ft (220 lb) aggregate

Brickwork
70–75 bricks
10 kg (22 lb) cement
40 kg or 1 cu ft (88 lb) sand
5 kg (11 lb) lime
OR 10 ml (⅓ fl oz) plasticizer

1 Although a strip foundation is sufficient for a small planter, it is easier to lay a concrete slab (in this case 100 mm [4 in] deep). To allow for drainage, place two bricks in the centre and remove before the concrete sets.
2 Peg and set up lines along the outside of two adjoining walls of the planter before you start laying the bricks. Make certain that the bricks are level and that

1

2

Above: *The planter has been finished off with paving bricks and any excess mortar removed with a metal scraper.*

the corners are at 90°, checking each one with a spirit level and a square.
3 An easy way to create weepholes for drainage is to exclude mortar at several of the vertical joints. This completed planter measures only 800 x 700 mm (2 ft 7 in x 2 ft 3 in), for which three weepholes are adequate. Piping can be inserted for more substantial drainage.

Continue laying bricks for six courses, checking to ensure your surfaces are level and plumb.

3

POOLS AND PONDS

POOLS AND PONDS CAN TRANSFORM THE MOST ORDINARY SETTING, GIVING IT A MAGICAL, TRANQUIL QUALITY. EVEN A VERY BEAUTIFUL SITE CAN BENEFIT FROM THE ADDITION OF A SPARKLING WATER FEATURE. WATER BRINGS LIFE, LIGHT, MOVEMENT AND REFLECTION, OFFERING A WONDERFUL CONTRAST TO PAVED SURFACES AND OTHER FIXED STRUCTURES. WHETHER IT IS CREATED IN A FORMAL OR NATURAL, OR ORNAMENTAL OR SIMPLE WAY, A WELL-PLANNED WATER FEATURE IS ALWAYS AESTHETICALLY APPEALING AND GUARANTEED TO DRAW VISITORS TO ITS EDGES.

LOCATION

The most important factor when planning a pond is its location. Eminently suitable are 'dead' corners, shady nooks which look as if they already fringe a pool, or areas with natural rocks and boulders.

Sometimes a slope where plants will not grow can be used successfully to make a tiered or flowing water feature, following the natural contours of the site. Exploit the fact that water flows downhill

Left: A half-raised pond built from random stone walling.

and collects in a low area and your pond will look natural and will blend in perfectly.

Trees provide welcome shade over a pond, but roots could damage the base and fallen leaves can look unsightly and cause problems. It is therefore preferable to site a pond in the open or under an evergreen tree.

STYLE

There are numerous ways of designing and creating ponds and water features, but the style you choose should be influenced by other existing features. Also take into consideration the full

extent of the area in which it will be located, since this will affect the type as well as size of your pond or pool.

While water features may, broadly speaking, be formal or informal, several other characteristics are as important. Decide whether you want to hear or only see the water; a still, mirror-like pond reflecting light can be as soothing as the sound of rushing or trickling water. If you simply want a visual feature, consider incorporating it in your patio design. It is true that moving water never fails to attract interest, enlivening any setting. It may be introduced as a fountain, which is usually quite formal and ornamental, or it could flow into a natural-looking

Above: *This formal raised pool incorporates a 'shell boy' fountain.*

waterfall (see picture on page 17).

If you decide on a fish pond, the kind of fish you choose will also affect your choice of construction. A Nishikigoi pond should be filtered so that you can see the brilliant colours of the fish. It should also be at least 600 mm (2 ft) deep and big enough to allow the fish to develop and grow. Try to create a variety of depths so that the koi can move between the cool depths and the warmer, shallow water. Goldfish, however, can survive happily in a small, shallow pool with no special

Pools and Ponds

equipment. They require little maintenance and so are often the best choice.

Introducing aquatic plants to oxygenate the water will prevent it from turning stagnant. Note that even if the water does become quite greenish, you do not have to replace it, as long as there are sufficient plants in the pond. In fish ponds, plants perform the additional functions of providing food and a spawning ground for the fish.

The water lily is the queen of all aquatic plants. It flowers throughout the summer and the large floating leaves keep the sunshine from the water, helping to control algae growth. Water lilies are best planted on the bottom of a pond – start by supporting them on bricks and they can be lowered gently as they grow.

There are four other types of plant you can have in a pond:

* *marginal plants* sit on a ledge at the edge of a pond to provide decoration. There is a wide and fascinating variety to choose from with both colourful flowers and leafy foliage.
* *deep marginals* are planted at the bottom of a pool to provide interest in the centre.
* *floating plants* are simply placed on the surface of the water and, like water lilies, help to control algae growth.
* *oxygenating plants* are essential to control algae. They are planted on the bottom of the pond and five bunches are needed for every square metre (10 sq ft) of water area.

Surprisingly, a water feature with plants requires only a few messy hours of cleaning in spring, when water plants that have grown too profusely should be taken out of the water, cut back and replanted.

Construction

Once you have decided on the type and style of pond you would like, you will have to choose your method of construction. The simplest way is to buy a ready-made shell, most commonly available in glassfibre-reinforced plastic (GRP or glassfibre), fibre-cement or high-density polyethylene. Some of these ready-made ponds can stand above ground, while others are designed to be sunken.

On the other hand, you can simply use heavy-duty plastic or synthetic rubber sheeting to line a hollow in the ground or you can build a more permanent structure in concrete or in brick, above or below the ground. This should be lined with plastic or sealed with a non-toxic bitumen (asphalt tar) sealant.

Our first step-by-step section features a simple, formal pond which is built of brick and sealed with non-toxic bitumen (asphalt tar), with its base below ground level and its sides extending above the paving surround.

Our second project shows a pond made using a heavy-duty liner with a crazy paving surround.

Sealing

The biggest and most common problem relating to pools and ponds is, appropriately enough, their ability to hold water. (How many leaking pools have been adapted to make sandpits for the children or filled in with earth and planted?) As always, meticulous preparation should avoid this problem.

Thick plastic or rubber sheeting will undoubtedly provide a waterproof lining, but it is fairly vulnerable to puncturing. In any case, its life-span is limited, and it will therefore have to be replaced periodically.

The interior surface of a masonry pond can be painted with a proprietary bitumen (asphalt tar) sealant, following the manufacturer's instructions. If brick is used, rendering (pargeting) it first will reduce the number of coats of bitumen (asphalt tar) required. Because of their dark colour, both black plastic and bitumen (asphalt tar) will give the pond a feeling of depth and mystery.

Left: *The effect of this circular brick pond has been cleverly enhanced by the leafy planter behind.*

1

2

3

4

DRAINAGE

While there are obvious advantages in constructing a pond with built-in drainage, deciding on a suitable water outlet may be a problem. Any plughole must be attached to a PVC pipe which should, in turn, feed into a drainage channel. This sometimes increases the likelihood of leaking, but thorough sealing around the hole with a good quality, flexible sealer can eliminate the problem. Most pumps will enable you to drain the pond from the top, thus avoiding the need for a plughole.

Alternatively, provided the base of your pond is higher than the surrounding ground, you can simply siphon all the water out with a piece of garden hose.

Step-by-step raised pond

The height from the foundation is 400 mm (16 in) and from the paving, which incorporates a slope for drainage, 200 to 230 mm (8 to 9 in). The foundation is 1,960 × 1,150 mm (6 ft 5 in × 3 ft 9 in) and varies from 150 mm (6 in) to 200 mm (8 in) deep at the edges. You will need:

Foundation

Concrete: 1:2½:3½ cement:sand: aggregate
50 kg (1 x 100 lb bag) cement
125 kg or 3 cu ft (276 lb) sand
200 kg or 4 cu ft (440 lb) aggregate

Above: *The pond filled with water.*

Brickwork

120–130 bricks
20–30 paving bricks
18 kg (40 lb) cement
108 kg or 2¾ cu ft (240 lb) builder's sand
9 kg (20 lb) lime
OR 8 ml (¾ fl oz) plasticizer

1 Mark the area of the proposed pond (see the section on square in Brickwork Principles, page 84), and excavate to the required depth. As this pond will extend above ground, incorporating a low brick wall, the excavated depth is about 300 mm (1 ft).
2 Mix the concrete (see page 87) and roughly line the bottom and sides of the hole.
3 Lay a foundation and build up a five-course wall topped with paving bricks, continually checking levels and corners.
4 If using plastic sheeting, spread this inside the pond when the first three courses are complete, finishing off with a further two courses and paving bricks. Otherwise, seal the pond with several coats of non-toxic bitumen (asphalt tar). When the bitumen (asphalt tar) sealant is dry, create areas of interest within the pond by placing rocks on the bottom and potted plants in groups on rocks near the surface.

Pools and Ponds

Step-by-step liner pond

The size and shape of pond you create is a matter of taste, but experience has shown that the minimum size to produce an attractive and clear pool and harmony between volume of water, plants and fish is around 4 sq m (40 sq ft).

The depth of the pond should be between 380 and 450 mm (15 to 18 in) for small to medium-sized ponds; 600 to 750 mm (24 to 30 in) for larger ponds (over 10 sq m or 100 sq ft). Build in shelves 230 mm (9 in) wide and 230 mm deep around the edge for marginal plants.

The pond shown here is constructed using a heavy-duty liner: for this, the sides of the pond should slope by approximately 20° – 75 mm (3 in) inwards for every 230 mm (9 in) of depth. To calculate the size of liner you need, take twice the maximum depth and add this to both the overall length and overall width of the pond, irrespective of the actual shape.

To build a 4 sq m (40 sq ft) pond, you will need:

Base
100 kg or 2½ cu ft (220 lb) builder's sand
Black plastic liner

Surround (600 mm [2 ft] wide)
5 sq m (50 sq ft) paving materials
40 kg or almost one bag (88 lb) cement
80 kg or 2 cu ft (176 lb) sand

1 Lay a hosepipe or rope to mark the size and shape of the pool you want, adjusting it until you are happy. Simple shapes with sweeping curves are best: avoid narrow necks, promontories, bays and inlets. Start excavating, cutting inside the marked outline to allow for final trimming later.
2 The shelves for marginal plants are cut out around the edges and the edges themselves trimmed back around 50 mm (2 in) to allow for the overlap of the edging stones.
3 Short wooden pegs are inserted about 1 m (3 ft 3 in) apart around the edge of pond and levelled with a spirit level – it
4 is vital that the top of the pond is

6

7

Above: In fine weather the pond edge makes a pleasant place to sit and relax.

horizontal as the water will soon show any discrepancies.

4 After final trimming and excavation, the depth and width of the marginal shelves (here two sets at different levels) should be checked and the inside of the pond inspected for any sharp stones or roots which could damage the liner.

5 A cushion of sand 12 mm (1/2 in) thick should be placed all over the excavated area, making sure it fills any holes. Smooth the sand down – at the top, make sure it is level with the marking pegs and then remove the pegs and fill the holes with more sand.

6 The pond liner is then draped loosely into the hole with an even overlap all the way round with stones or blocks placed at the corners and, if necessary, on the sides. Start filling with water.

7 As the pond fills, the stones should be eased off at intervals to allow the liner to fit snugly into the hole. Some creasing is inevitable, but some creases can be removed by stretching and fitting as the pond fills.

8 When the pool is full, cut off the excess liner, leaving a flap around 100 to 125 mm (4 to 5 in) wide. This can be temporarily secured to prevent slipping by driving some 100 mm (4 in) nails

8

9

through it into the ground.

9 Rectangular pools can be edged with pre-cast regular paving: curved ponds are better finished with broken stone flags or concrete paving stones as used in crazy paving. Lay the edging stones on a mortar of one part cement to three parts sand, removing the temporary nails from the liner as you go.

10 Ideally, the pond should be emptied and refilled before planting and stocking with fish – especially if any mortar has been dropped in during the construction. Add fountains, lights and other ornaments – here, a small geyser jet has been used which will not disturb the water lilies or other marginal plants.

10

POOLS AND PONDS
PUMPS FOR PONDS

A variety of pumps is available for use with fish ponds and ornamental pools. Choose one which will cope with the water capacity of your pond and which will also power a waterfall or fountain. You should also make certain that the unit will enable you to pump water from the pond, thus draining it when necessary. Relatively small in size, pumps suitable for ponds must be specially designed for the purpose with a completely sealed motor housing so that they can be submerged in the water.

Pumps are available in both mains voltage and extra low-voltage (typically 24V versions). Mains-voltage pumps need an outside electricity supply, the installation of which is a job best left to a professional electrician. ('Mains-voltage' means 240 V in the UK and 110 V in the US.) Low-voltage pumps are supplied from a transformer. For ponds close to the house, this can be plugged in to a convenient power point inside the house and low-voltage cable led to the position of the pond. For more distant ponds, a mains-voltage supply can be taken overhead or underground to the position of the pond where the transformer will need to be placed in a waterproof shed next to the pond.

Most pond pumps will provide a variety of fountain patterns (the fountain can be mounted on top of the pump or can be a separate feature) and can be used, separately or simultaneously, to power a waterfall.

LIGHTS

Once you have installed electricity at the site of the pond, you can add lighting to enhance its appearance at night.

Low-voltage lights can be placed around the pond or special types can be floated on the surface (or, if weighted, under the surface) for a more dramatic effect.

The clever combination of lighting and fountains can create particularly spectacular night-time effects.

Fountain jets

Pond fountain jets fall into four basic types. These are shown above (reading clockwise from top left).

The simple spray jet varies in size and can have as many as three fountains.

The bell jet produces a clear dome of flowing water.

The foam jet is a powerful geyser, which seems to be in constant motion.

The tulip jet creates an endlessly elegant spout of water.

Above: *An attractive waterfall feature produced using a pond pump. The colourful and exotic plants add to the tropical effect.*

Right: *This miniature pond, which blends cleverly with the wall behind, has been enhanced by a lion's mask fountain.*

Left: *The dramatic, crimson water lilies and 'rock baby' fountain have given this raised pond a touch of grandeur and made it more interesting.*

Far left: *Creative lighting, especially with coloured lights, can give your pond a magical quality at night.*

Seat and Table

Built-in outdoor furniture simplifies seating for outdoor entertaining, takes up little room, and adds to the value of your home. Instead of having to move chairs and tables outside whenever you want a meal or a quiet drink in the fresh air, the basic equipment is already there. All you need do is add cushions for comfort.

Location

The design of furniture and its location will depend on your requirements. If you want a place to sit and relax or read, away from the hustle and bustle of normal household activities, you will probably want a simple yet comfortable bench tucked away in a quiet corner. But if you plan to use the furniture for entertaining or for family meals, it will have to meet entirely different needs.

Built-in seats and tables may be combined with other built-in features. The most common location for this type of furniture is on patios, especially when barbecues and other outdoor cooking facilities are included. Other spots where people congregate regularly, for example paved areas around ponds or pools, are obvious sites for both benches and tables.

The furniture itself may blend in naturally or, if attractive and unusual, may become a striking feature. A tiled or mosaic seat, for instance, adds interest as well as providing a place to rest.

Materials

Any furniture left outdoors permanently should be made from weather-proof materials. Brick and stone are certainly very durable, but do not provide particularly comfortable surfaces for seating, and therefore need to be finished off with a more agreeable material.

Wood is a good option for table tops and seats, and it can look very attractive combined with brick. Alternatively, a practical table can be made by topping a stocky pillar with a smooth, pre-cast concrete slab. Keep bricklaying to a minimum by building a bench alongside a

Above: *The perfect setting for a relaxed meal outside.*

retaining or screen wall, with the wall forming the backrest, and timber slats forming the seat.

Step-by-step seat and table
For this project a raft or slab foundation was used, covering the base of the whole area of the structure. This type of foundation is not as deep as a strip foundation, which is used to build walls. For this project the foundation was 2,100 × 1,700 mm (6 ft 11 in × 5 ft 7 in) and 100 mm (4 in) deep. You will need:

Foundation
75 kg (165 lb) cement
200 kg or 5 cu ft (440 lb) sand
300 kg or 6 cu ft (662 lb) aggregate

Brickwork
410–450 bricks
66 kg (1½ x 100 lb bags) cement
396 kg or 10 cu ft (873 lb) sand
33 kg (73 lb) lime
OR 66 ml (2 fl oz) plasticizer
11 pieces of wood, 150 x 38 mm (6 x 1½ in) (length for table 4 x 1,800 mm [5 ft 11 in], 2 x 570 mm [22 in]; for seat 3 x 1,550 mm [5 ft 1 in], 2 x 420 mm [16½ in])
22 x No. 8 x 75 mm (3 in) coach screws (screwspikes) (12 for table, 10 for seat)

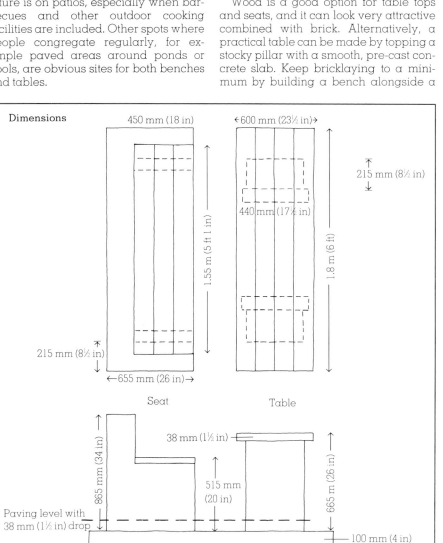

Dimensions

450 mm (18 in)

600 mm (23½ in)

215 mm (8½ in)

440 mm (17½ in)

1.55 m (5 ft 1 in)

1.8 m (6 ft)

215 mm (8½ in)

655 mm (26 in)

Seat

Table

38 mm (1½ in)

865 mm (34 in)

515 mm (20 in)

665 m (26 in)

Paving level with 38 mm (1½ in) drop

100 mm (4 in)

1.9 m (6 ft 3 in)

2

3

1

4

1 Peg out the area required for your seat and table, allowing an extra 100 to 200 mm (4 to 8 in) on all four sides to accommodate the slab foundation. Excavate to a depth of 100 mm (4 in) – about the depth of a brick on edge. Make sure your surface is level before you mix the concrete and lay the foundation. Check the levels by placing a brick at each corner and using a spirit level placed on a long straight-edge.

2 Mix cement, sand and aggregate in a ratio of 1:2½:3½. Spread the concrete over the entire area, levelling with the back of a spade. You can leave the bricks in the corners to help keep the concrete surface level.

3 Once the concrete is dry, lay a one-brick wall for the seat. Use the straight-edge and the spirit level to keep the back wall level. Check with the builder's square that all corners are at 90°.

4 Now build up two courses at the corners, using the spirit level to check both horizontal and vertical surfaces. Use a gauge rod to make certain that the brick courses are regular.

5 Start building up the two pillars which will support the wooden table top. It is easiest and most practicable to work on the bench and table simultaneously, gradually building up all the walls.

Stretcher bond (see page 62) is used for these two features which both have wooden strip surfaces. From the

foundation level, the seat back is built up to 11 courses, the seat itself to seven courses and the table up to nine courses. When planning your final levels, take into account that nearly two of these courses may be below the final paving.

Strips of wood are screwed together and fitted across the walls which form the built-in seat. Thinner brick pavers are used to finish off the top and ends of the seating section, as the wood does not extend to the edges. The table is built in a similar way, but with an extra piece of wood. The cross pieces are cut to slot in on the inside of the two piers, to prevent the table top from sliding from side to side and to reinforce the seat.

5

Barbecues

When the weather is fine, nothing beats cooking and eating outside. A permanent and well-constructed barbecue provides an effective way for a family or group of friends to socialize while cooking an informal meal. A simple built-in barbecue, maintenance-free and weather-proof, is easy to construct and the enjoyment it will afford you is certainly worth the effort.

Location

The location of any barbecue is a vital factor. Careful thought and planning will provide a pleasant entertainment area which you can exploit to the full. Lack of forethought and inadequate attention to factors such as sun, wind, accessibility to the house and the nearness of neighbours are more likely to result in wasted time, effort and money.

Spend time sitting in various parts of the site and take note of climate-related factors. Take note of the areas that receive hardly any sun or are particularly wind-swept. You are unlikely to want to end up cooking at the barbecue on your own, while guests sit elsewhere. The ideal spot should offer both sunshine and some shade, as well as shelter from the prevailing wind, so that guests can relax around the barbecue.

It is often preferable to site a barbecue near the house to avoid tedious trips to the kitchen for food, water and utensils. However, if it is too near, you may end up with discoloured walls and a smoke-filled house whenever you cook outside. It could also be a fire hazard.

Patios often make good barbecue sites, but if you opt for an established area which is enclosed or covered, construct a properly designed chimney to channel smoke away.

Design

Before considering the design options of a barbecue, determine your needs and those of family and friends who will make regular use of the area. Evaluate your life-style and choose your design to suit it.

Even the simplest barbecue arrangement should have both adequate working surfaces and convenient storage space for those cooking utensils you will use most frequently, as well as for wood and charcoal.

If you cannot afford everything you would like to incorporate at the time of building, plan your barbecue for future improvement or expansion, allowing for additional features at a later date. These could include built-in seating and tables, fitted doors for the storage space, or planters to add colour.

The style of the structure – including seating and other additional features – should blend with your home and complement existing building materials. Match brick, render (parget) and paint and take care that the barbecue does not dominate existing features.

Barbecues may be built with brick, concrete walling blocks or stone; they may be mass-produced or portable; regarding fuel, they may use wood, charcoal or gas.

The advantages of built-in barbecues include convenience, durability and, provided they are imaginatively designed and well-built, an increase in the value of your property.

Design options are endless, and range from simple, functional units, such as the unit for which we have given building instructions, to elaborate designs incorporating grills; simple spits or even rotisseries; pizza and baking ovens, as well as seating and storage facilities.

Foundation

A sturdy foundation is an important factor when building a barbecue. Its depth will, of course, depend on the size and weight of the structure it will support. A smallish unit can be built on a raft or slab foundation 75 to 100 mm (3 to 4 in) deep (see *Seat and Table*, page 18). For this reason, an existing patio will often present a suitable base, provided it is level and firm.

For easy cleaning and drainage, the foundation should be sloped slightly towards the front of the barbecue.

Construction

Mark out the area for your barbecue and excavate an extra 100 to 200 mm (4 to 8 in) on each side. If you are working alongside an existing patio, mark the paving as an additional guide.

Right: *The simple style of this barbecue makes it an excellent project for any do-it-yourself enthusiast who wants to build a basic yet practical structure. The slatted wooden doors and wooden seat were later additions.*

Barbecues

During bricklaying, check levels and surfaces constantly, using a straight-edge and spirit level, adding or removing mortar from under the bricks if necessary. Place the spirit level diagonally against the bricks as well as in a horizontal and a vertical position. Use a square to check corners, and use corner blocks with a builder's line to help maintain a straight edge. If you find that any bricks are lying skew, tap them gently into place. Scrape off any excess mortar as you work.

Step-by-step barbecue

The base measurements for this barbecue are: 1,800 × 525 mm (5 ft 11 × 20½ in) with a foundation 2,000 × 800 mm (6 ft 7 × 2 ft 7 in) and 100 mm (4 in) deep. The materials you will need to build the barbecue are:

Foundation

Concrete mixture: 1:2½:3½ cement:sand: aggregate
50 kg (1 × 100 lb bag) cement
125 kg or 3 cu ft (276 lb) builder's sand
200 kg or 4 cu ft (440 lb) aggregate

Barbecue unit

240 bricks (30 halved)
53 paving bricks (1 halved)
75 kg (165 lb) cement
300 kg or 7½ cu ft (662 lb) builder's sand
38 kg (84 lb) builder's lime
OR 75 ml (2½ fl oz) plasticizer

4 standard concrete lintels, 1,500 mm (4 ft 11 in) long
8 round iron pegs OR 100 mm (4 in) bolts
450 x 450 mm (18 in square) grid, for cooking

1 Having marked out the area, excavate to the depth of one brick on edge and lay a foundation using concrete mixed to a ratio of 1:2½:3½ (cement:sand:aggregate).
2 When the concrete has set, lay the first course of bricks without mortar and mark pencil lines on the concrete. Remove the bricks. Mix mortar in the ratio of 1:1:6 (cement:lime:sand).
3 Using the pencil markings as a guide, lay a sausage-like bed of mortar, 10 to 12 mm (½ in) thick and about 100 mm (4 in) wide, along the lines where each wall of the barbecue will be built. Use lines and furrows (see page 89) to lay the bricks.
4 Using the line and furrow in the mortar as a guide, follow the pattern shown when the bricks were laid without mortar and lay the first course of bricks which form the two side walls of the structure (10 bricks in all). Use corner blocks and check levels frequently with a spirit level.
5 Now lay the long outer wall and then lay the bricks which will form the two short inner walls. Once again, use the spirit level and square frequently. All

gaps between bricks should be filled in with mortar before you begin to lay the second course of bricks.
6 The stretcher bond used for this barbecue requires six half bricks for every second course. Begin laying at the outside corners of the back wall, but before you set the first brick of the second course in place, lay a strip of mortar on top of the first course of bricks. Build up both outer corners to three courses before starting on the second course of the straight walls. To complete the inside corner of the second course, put a half brick in place. Fill in any gaps with mortar before placing a full brick in position to complete the inside corner of the third course.
7 Continue laying the bricks for a total of 10 courses. Lay a single course of bricks around the outside edges of the structure and four pre-cast concrete lintels across the top of the inside bricks. Spread mortar over the lintels and then build up walls to shield the cooking area.
8 Set bolts into the wall to support a grid. Rake out any excess mortar on the external walls. Thinner brick pavers are used for the final course of bricks on all surfaces, including the floor surface below the barbecue. An alternative option is to build up a last course of bricks over the lintels and then to tile the working surfaces on each side of the cooking area.

2

5

6

8

STEPS AND STAIRWAYS

STEPS – WHETHER BUILT OF BRICK, STONE, CONCRETE BLOCK, SOLID CONCRETE OR A COMBINATION OF MATERIALS – HAVE A CERTAIN WAY OF ADDING CHARM AND INTEREST TO AN OUTDOOR AREA. A FLIGHT OF STEPS IS HIGHLY PRACTICAL ON A SLOPING PROPERTY – PROVIDING SAFE AND EASY ACCESS TO INACCESSIBLE OR INFREQUENTLY VISITED AREAS. STEPS ARE ESSENTIAL ON STEEPLY SLOPING SITES, IF ONLY TO ALLOW ACCESS BETWEEN THE BOUNDARY AND FRONT ENTRANCE OF THE HOUSE.

AS WELL AS HAVING A PRACTICAL PURPOSE, STEPS CAN SERVE A DECORATIVE FUNCTION, BECOMING A FEATURE IN THEMSELVES. ALTHOUGH IT MIGHT SEEM AN AMBITIOUS TASK, BUILDING STEPS IS NOT AS DIFFICULT AS YOU MIGHT EXPECT, PROVIDED YOU OBSERVE A FEW BASIC RULES.

LOCATION AND DESIGN

The style and design of steps depends largely on their location and their intended use. It is always very important to plan your steps carefully. Make certain they will be located practically and to the best visual advantage before you start building. Whether their use is practical or decorative, steps should have some sense of purpose.

You may find that the slope in your plot does not make steps a necessity, but consider the decorative aspect. A gradually stepped pathway could, for instance, become a feature on its own. If possible, avoid making a long flight of stairs follow a straight line.

Plants on either side will enhance any flight of steps. Use trailing greenery or flowering, ground-covering plants to soften stark lines or build planters for dramatic, bold specimens (see our step-by-step project). For a charmingly whimsical effect, you could plant sweet-smelling herbs between the spaced treads of informal steps.

MATERIALS

Whatever style of steps you decide on – be it formal brick or rustic stone – it is important that they enhance your property rather than conflict with existing features. For instance, if your house has a very distinctive style, it might be best to treat steps leading to the front door as an extension of the building, and use materials which blend with or reflect its style of architecture. On the other hand, continuing the colour and texture of existing pathways or paving could be equally effective.

A popular choice for outdoor steps is concrete paving slabs for the treads laid on brick or block walls as the risers. A typical method of construction is shown in the drawing – the bottom riser is built on a concrete base, the space behind filled

Below: *A standard method of constructing steps with pavers and brick risers.*

Below right and detail: *Formwork needs to be constructed for solid concrete steps.*

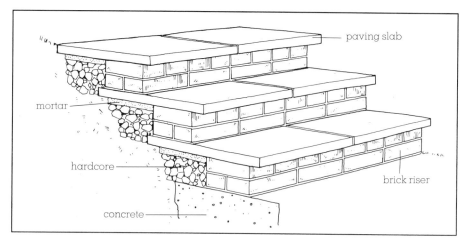

paving slab

mortar

hardcore

concrete

brick riser

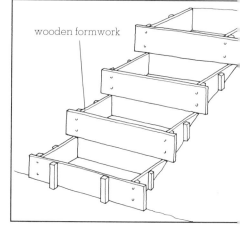

wooden formwork

with hardcore and earth and the paving slab then laid on a bed of mortar across the riser and the hardcore. The second riser is then built on top of the paving slab and so on to the top of the flight.

Steps can be made entirely from brick, as in our first step-by-step example, or can be built from concrete blocks bedded in sand, as in our second example.

To build solid concrete steps, formwork needs to be constructed for each of the steps. Concrete is poured in for the bottom step, levelled off and allowed to set until firm enough to take the weight of the second step.

A popular and particularly practical material for constructing steps is paving bricks. Consider, however, combining brick with other materials to add textural interest – treads of concrete paving blocks or tiles; or perhaps incorporating railway sleeper (railroad tie) ends.

The instructions given for building steps with brick are a general guide, and the same method may be applied when using bricks in combination with concrete paving blocks, regular-cut slate or crazy paving.

EXCAVATION

Once you have decided where to site the steps and what materials to use, mark out the area with a profile (see diagram) and excavate. You should try to avoid cutting bricks and should therefore take the size of the bricks, pavers and slabs you are using (plus mortar where necessary) into account when choosing the size of the steps, especially the risers (see table).

If you build on a steep bank, you will probably have to construct side retaining walls first (see page 68). Failure to do this could result in erosion and eventual collapse of the steps. Be sure to measure the width of your stairway first.

Left: *Bricks seem the obvious choice for the steps leading up to this house.*

Below: *Here a dramatic effect has been created by building steps over an arch.*

tamping beam

HEIGHT

The rise of a step should not exceed 200 mm (8 in), while the length of a tread should be at least 250 mm (10 in). Outdoor steps are, however, often much more gradual than this.

As a rule, the higher each step, the brisker your pace will be as you walk up and down them. Long, shallow steps invite a leisurely stroll. Steps planned for the garden or backyard will therefore be less steep than, say, a stairway providing access to the entrance of your home. If your plot is very spacious, the gradient of your steps can be as gradual as 1 in 15. A long gradual slope may look better with a series of steps, rather than with a single stairway. Alternatively, break the steps with planters or seating.

TREADS AND RISERS

The relationship between the length of the tread and the height of the riser between treads is important since they must be in proportion to each other. The more gradual the slope and the longer the tread, the shallower the riser should be.

Some successful combinations may be used as a guide; for instance, a tread which is 300 mm (12 in) long works well with a 175 mm (7 in) riser, while a 500 mm (20 in) tread should be combined with a shallower 100 mm (4 in) riser.

Above: *Green vegetation in the planters sets off the red of the brickwork.*

WIDTH

Ideally, garden steps should be 1.2 to 1.5 m (4 to 5 ft) wide, which is wide enough for two people to walk comfortably abreast. Functional steps built purely for access should be at least 600 mm (2 ft)

Recommended tread/riser combinations

Tread length	Riser height	Possible riser materials
500 mm (20 in)	100 mm (4 in)	one course of bricks plus 25 mm (1 in) paving slab
450 mm (18 in)	115 mm (4½ in)	one course of bricks on edge or one course of bricks + 38 mm (1½ in) slab
400 mm (16 in)	140 mm (5½ in)	one course of concrete-based walling blocks + 38 mm (1½ in) slab
350 mm (14 in)	150 mm (6 in)	two courses of brick laid flat
300 mm (12 in)	175 mm (7 in)	two courses of brick + 25 mm (1 in) slab

wide. To prevent puddles forming, steps should be given a gentle slope of, say, 1 in 100 (5 mm/500 mm or ¼ in/4 ft).

PROFILES

To measure the depth of your slope and to establish exactly how many steps will fit, it is advisable to make a simple profile device with two straight-edged pieces of wood joined at right angles. The vertical must be placed at the point where the steps should end, and the horizontal at the top of the steps. Place a spirit level on the horizontal plank to ensure your profile levels are straight. The depth of the slope is the distance along the horizontal section of the profile, A-C, while the vertical section indicates the total change in level, A-B.

Use these figures to decide the best number of steps. For example, if (as shown) the total length is 1.2 m (4 ft) and the total height is 420 mm (1 ft 4½ in), you might think of having two, three or four steps. Two would give too great a riser (210 mm or 8¼ in); four would give steps with 105 mm (4 in) risers but a tread length of only 300 mm (1 ft), which is too short for this combination. So the best choice is three steps, 140 mm (5½ in) high and 400 mm (16 in) long.

It may sometimes be necessary to change the extent of the depth of the slope to enable you to fit in steps which

Brickwork
72 bricks
56 brick pavers
15 kg (33 lb) cement
60 kg or 1½ cu ft (132 lb) sand
8 kg (18 lb) lime
OR 15 ml (½ fl oz) plasticizer

1 Establish the level of both the top and bottom step by using your profile and set up a building line as a guide. It is not necessary to dig away all the earth. Simply cut out the general shape.
2 Lay a concrete foundation 50 mm (2 in) thick and to the length and width of your tread. When this is dry, lay your first course using bricklaying mortar. In this case, the first step will be an extension of the path, so only paving bricks are laid.
3 Fill in the gap behind the tread with concrete, to the level of your paving bricks. This new concrete base will form the foundation for your second step. Once it is dry, you can start laying the riser.
4 Now build up the riser (here with two courses of brick) behind the first tread, using corner blocks and a builder's line to ensure that the bricks are laid straight. Use your spirit level to ensure that the bricks are level and vertical.
5 Fill in the gap behind the bricks with concrete, extending into a level 'platform' for the tread pavers. When this is dry, lay the pavers on a bed of mortar, using the spirit level frequently.

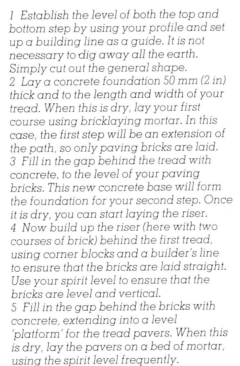

conform satisfactorily to the tread/riser proportions required and to suit the size of your bricks (plus mortar) or other materials.

Step-by-step steps
For three steps 900 mm (3 ft) wide with 200 mm (8 in) risers and 290 mm (11½ in) treads, you will need:

Foundation
10 kg or ⅕ bag (22 lb) cement
30 kg or 1 cu ft (66 lb) sand
45 kg or 1 cu ft (100 lb) aggregate

Below: *A simple profile for building steps.*

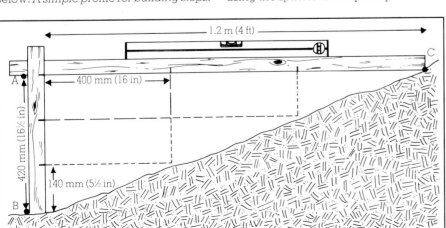

Step-by-step concrete block steps

For three steps 1,800 mm (6 ft) wide with 200 mm (8 in) risers and 500 mm (20 in) treads, you will need:

55 curbstones
110 concrete paving blocks

Foundation/sub-base
35 kg or ⅔ bag (77 lb) cement
90 kg or 2¼ cu ft (200 lb) sand
140 kg or 3 cu ft (308 lb) aggregate
100 kg or 2½ cu ft (220 lb) concreting sand
200 kg or 4 cu ft (440 lb) hardcore

1 Start with two side brick walls and the site roughly excavated.
2 Wooden formwork is used to form the concrete for the riser curbstones. This must be correctly positioned, levelled and secured.
3 Concrete is shovelled into the formwork and roughly levelled off.
4 Once the concrete has set (allow three days or more), remove the formwork.
5 Use a string line to position the curbstones and place them on a mortar bed.
6 Lay all the curbstones.
7 Now shovel in a mixture of small stones and finer granular material.
8 Compact the sub-base thoroughly until it is at the required depth (add more material if necessary).
9 Shovel fine concreting sand in and compact this with the hand compactor. Lay two screeding rails 60 mm (2½ in) below the finished step height.
10 Screed off the sand and remove the screeding rails.
11 Use a block splitter (masonry saw) to cut blocks for filling in small gaps.
12 Lay the paving blocks in the required pattern – here basketweave.
13 Compact the sand by tamping down with the hand compactor, using wood to protect the block surface.
14 Brush fine sand across the blocks, making sure it gets into all the joints.
15 Compact again to force sand in between the joints and to level the blocks.
16 A fine set of steps.

8

11

14

9

12

15

10

13

16

Arches

WHILE SOLID WALLS PROVIDE PRIVACY AND PROTECTION, THE INCLUSION OF ARCHES AT ENTRANCES OR OTHER POINTS OF ACCESS CAN ADD VISUAL INTEREST AND A PLEASING NEW DIMENSION TO THE DESIGN OF YOUR GARDEN OR BACKYARD.

Location

Arches may be introduced into the design in several ways – to frame an entrance, add interest to a plain wall or to provide a framework for fragrant flowering climbers. It is not usually advisable to construct a single arch – unless it has a definite sense of purpose it will simply look out of place. So, in the planning stages, decide whether your arch will bridge a functional opening, separate sections of the plot or offer support for plants to trail over.

An arch can be introduced to frame an opening in a wall, as an extension, rising above a wall, or as a free-standing structure. Whichever type is used, it should mirror any other arches within view. These may recur within the wall itself, perhaps as a second utility entrance, or be incorporated in the shape of nearby structures such as garage doors, a patio wall, window frames or the entrance to the house itself.

Small-scale arches may also be included in your design. They can be used to frame a postbox, a refuse bin (garbage can) or a nook.

Construction

Building an archway is a project that needs to be tackled very carefully, particularly if it is to span a wide opening. The most widely accepted method is to work with a supporting formwork (also called former or a turning-piece), which is cut in the shape of a semicircle or arc or, where a less pronounced effect is desired, as a smaller segment of a circle (a segmental arch).

A semicircular arch is generally simpler to set out and to build – a segmental arch means some geometrical drawing

Below: *An arch built into a wall is an unusual way to frame features such as this gargoyle fountain.*

and the wall bricks on either side have to be shaped to take the first arch bricks (which will not be horizontal). The formwork may be made up of two pieces of chipboard or plywood nailed together, but separated with blocks of wood around the edges. This is positioned where the arch is to be constructed, and bricks are then laid over it.

Formwork for Semicircular Arches

The formula for setting out an arch in a semicircle is simple: half the span of the opening is equal to the rise of the arch.

and then use it as a template to cut a second piece.

Now lay one cut-out piece of board flat and line the inside edges with blocks of wood, approximately the same thickness (less the thickness of the boards) as the wall. Cover with the second piece of board and nail this to each block; then turn over the board and attached blocks, and nail on the remaining board. Cover the edge with a strip of hardboard, nailing to secure.

FORMWORK FOR

SEGMENTAL ARCHES

While designed along the same principles as a semicircular arch, a segmental arch will give a less pronounced curve. When making the formwork for such an arch, it is sensible to include a little extra below the baseline of the rise, for ease of handling.

The first step is to decide on the height of the riser, which should never be less than a sixth of the span (for the purpose of this explanation, 900 mm [3 ft]). Lay out the board and draw a straight 900 mm (3 ft) baseline from A to B (see diagram). Mark the centre point and draw a second line at right angles through it. Measure the height of your rise (150 mm [6 in]) from the same centre point and mark C. Draw a line from A to C, bisect and draw another perpendicular line through the new centre point. The point at which it intersects your original perpendicular line, E, is the base point for drawing a segment of your circle, using the method described for semicircular arches.

Note that if your rise had been 250 mm (10 in) to F, G would then mark the base point for drawing the circle.

BUILDING THE ARCH

While the construction of an archway may seem like a formidable task, it is possible for a novice bricklayer to master the skills required by systematically following a few basic rules.

Once the formwork has been made it is placed in position in the wall opening and is supported by a timber framework constructed from pieces of wood at least 100 x 50 mm (4 x 2 in). Pairs of wedges are placed under the framework to ensure that the formwork is absolutely level at the correct height (these will also help when it comes to getting the formwork out once the arch has been built).

If the former has not been marked with the brick positions before putting it in place, these can be marked by laying the bricks 'dry' with wedges in between to represent the mortar courses. If you are continuing upwards with the wall over the arch, check with a gauge rod that the top of the keystone will line up with the first full course of bricks.

Above: A striking arch which adds visual interest to the gate while providing a framework for the plants to grow over.

Right: This diagram shows how to set out a segmental arch geometrically.

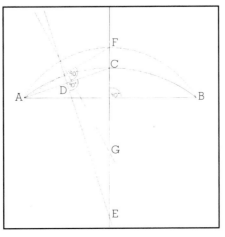

The base of the completed formwork must be equal in width to the span and must line up with (and therefore mark) the baseline of the rise.

To draw the shape, lay your board flat on the ground and mark out a semicircle with a pencil attached to a piece of string, measuring the rise as half the width of the span. Cut out the shape with a jigsaw

1

2

3

4

It is best to build up the arch evenly from both sides to prevent it being pushed out of position – as you lay the bricks, check that they are in the correct place (i.e. lined up with the marks on the former) and use a spirit level (or straight-edge) to ensure that each face of the arch is level with the faces of the former.

The last block to go into place is the 'keystone' at the very top of the arch. Make sure this is firmly in place and leave the mortar to dry for at least three days before removing the former.

Step-by-step arch

To make the formwork, you will need:

1,200 mm (3 ft 11 in) chipboard
50 mm (2 in) square wood, cut into a 1.2 m (4 ft) length
Strip of hardboard, whose width equals the thickness of the arch and whose length is 1:6 times the arch width
75 mm (3 in) wire nails to nail chipboard and blocks together
40 mm (1½ in) wire nails to nail hardboard onto formwork

Bricks/blocks

Apart from a separate keystone, you can use the same bricks or blocks that you are using for building the wall to make the arch.

1 Using one of the two methods described, draw the shape of your formwork onto the board and cut out two with a jigsaw.
2 Cut the square length of wood into six blocks, each 190 mm (7½ in) long, and nail these in place between the two pieces of board.
3 Cut a strip of hardboard to fit the perimeter of the arc and nail it on to the wooden blocks lining the edge of the formwork. This will give you a smooth and continuous surface over which the bricks can be laid.
4 Using the gauge rod, work out the position of the blocks to be laid over the top of the formwork. Avoid having to cut blocks by making mortar joints slightly thicker than usual, if necessary. Mark the formwork as a guide.
5 Before the arch former is made, the wall needs to be built up to the level of the bottom of the arch – here with concrete blocks.
6 Wedges can be used to position the blocks around the former so that the lines can be drawn back to the centre of the circle showing the position of each of the blocks.
7 Blocks are laid in mortar from either side, checking all the time that they have the correct alignment and are level with the face of the former.
8 The last block to go into place is the keystone – here one three courses deep and standing slightly proud of the surrounding blockwork for effect.

7

8

33

PILLARS AND PIERS

FREE-STANDING BLOCK AND CONCRETE BLOCK PILLARS AND PIERS HAVE VARIOUS USES, INCLUDING ACTING AS SUPPORTS FOR BASIC PERGOLAS OR ARBORS, AS POSTS FOR GATES AND DRIVEWAY ENTRANCES, AS BASES FOR SUNDIALS OR BIRD BATHS AND AS ESSENTIAL UPRIGHTS WHICH FORM THE SUPPORTING STRUCTURES FOR CARPORTS. INTERMEDIATE OR END PIERS ARE PUT IN FREE-STANDING BRICK WALLS FOR ESSENTIAL ADDITIONAL SUPPORT. BUILDING A PILLAR OR PIER IS RELATIVELY EASY ONCE YOU HAVE ACQUIRED THE BASIC SKILLS OF BRICKLAYING AND UNDERSTOOD THE BASIC METHODS OF CONSTRUCTION.

FOUNDATION

The minimum foundation depth for a brick pillar is 200 mm (8 in) although it may be advisable to make it as deep as 600 mm (2 ft), depending on its height and the weight (if any) it will carry.

The concrete mix used for a small pad foundation of this kind should be the standard 1:2½:3½ mix. This mixture was used for the pillar in our step-by-step project since it was less than a metre (3 ft 3in) high and its purpose was to be decorative rather than supportive.

REINFORCING

Some pillars must be built to take a considerable load, like those which are part of a carport and support the weight of a roof. They should also be able to withstand the force of wind gusting underneath the roof. For this reason both reinforcing rods and a strong mortar mix should be used in their construction.

Of course, any roof structure must also be securely fixed to a pillar and metal reinforcement should be built into the final five courses.

When building brick piers and pillars, it is usually advisable to incorporate vertical metal reinforcing rods. One or two rods are set in the centre of the foundation and propped up with timber while the concrete dries. The bricks are then laid around the rods, and additional mortar is used to fill in the central cavity as you work. It is advisable to let the mortar set for seven days if the pillar is to support a roof or covering of some sort.

For tall pillars or piers, embed a 'starter rod' into the foundation concrete and then tie further reinforcing rods to this with galvanized wire.

BUILDING PILLARS AND PIERS

It is best to make free-standing pillars out of an even number of bricks, whether they are solid or hollow, and to make them square. Intermediate or end piers in walls can be an odd number of brick sizes – a hollow square pier, with sides the width of three bricks, is a popular choice in half-brick walls, for example.

With piers in or on walls, there is a choice between bonding the brickwork of the pier to the bonding system of the wall

Left: Brick pillars have been used here to support a wooden pergola over a patio area. The same technique could also be employed to build a carport.

Above: *In long high walls like this one movement joints and supporting piers need to be placed at regular intervals.*

Right: *The brickwork of the pier has been bonded to the half-brick wall.*

Below: *Expanded metal used to reinforce the joint between piers and wall.*

Bottom left: *Movement or control joint. Half of the metal strip has been greased to prevent a bond.*

Left: *'Starter rod' reinforcement is required for tall pillars and piers. The starter rod is concreted in place.*

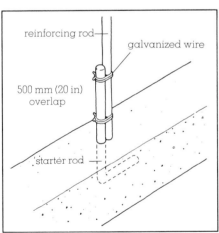

reinforcing rod

galvanized wire

500 mm (20 in) overlap

'starter rod'

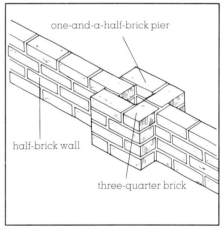

one-and-a-half-brick pier

half-brick wall

three-quarter brick

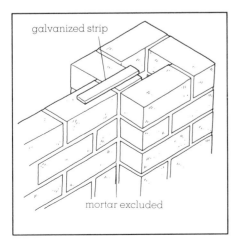

galvanized strip

mortar excluded

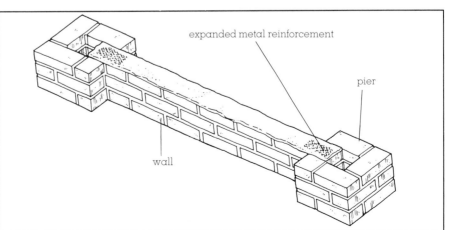

expanded metal reinforcement

pier

wall

PILLARS AND PIERS

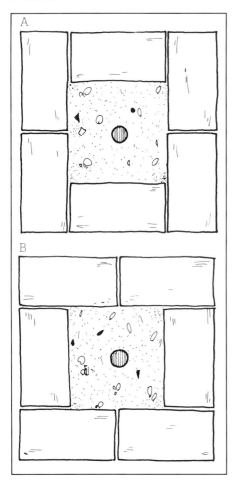

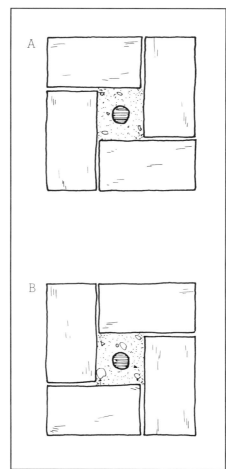

Left: *The diagram shows the brick courses for pillars and piers. Lay one course as in A, one as in B, one as in A and so on until the full height is achieved. This ensures proper bonding.*

or cutting bricks in half in alternate courses and leaving a vertical joint at the sides of the pier and reinforcing the horizontal courses with expanded metal or wall ties.

Leaving a vertical joint has the advantage that it can be used to create a movement (or 'control') joint in longer walls. Here, mortar is left out of the vertical joint and a flat strip of galvanized metal laid in the horizontal joints with one half of it lightly greased. This allows the wall to expand and contract along its length but supports the wall in a sideways direction. The sides of the otherwise open vertical joint are filled with non-setting mastic.

Step-by-step pillar
To build a hollow four-brick pillar, 900 mm (3 ft) high (excluding brick pavers), with a foundation 600 × 400 mm (2 ft × 16 in) and 110 mm (4½ in) deep, the materials you will need are:

Foundation
10 kg or ⅛ bag (22 lb) cement
25 kg or ½ cu ft (55 lb) sand
40 kg or 1 cu ft (66 lb) aggregate

Brickwork
50 bricks
5 brick pavers
10 kg (22 lb) cement
40 kg or 1 cu ft (88 lb) builder's sand
5 kg (11 lb) lime
OR 10 ml (⅓ fl oz) plasticizer
Metal reinforcing rod, about 1 m (3 ft 3 in) long

Render
8 kg (18 lb) cement
48 kg or 1¼ cu ft (106 lb) builder's sand
4 kg (9 lb) lime
OR 8 ml (¼ fl oz) plasticizer

1 An area of 600 x 600 mm (2 ft sq) must be excavated for a free-standing four-brick course pillar such as this, but this pier is attached to the wall and was built at the same time. The foundation must be laid first and allowed to dry thoroughly. Set out the first course of bricks without mortar.
2 It is essential to ensure that the four corners of the pillar are at exactly 90° to each other. Once you have laid the first course, check the corners with a builder's square. As you work, remember to check the height with a gauge rod and to use a spirit level to

ensure each course is level and plumb.
3 A reinforcing rod is inserted into the still-wet mortar which has been poured into the central cavity of the pier. The top of the rod extends to the finished level of the wall and the pier. To keep it from falling over, prop up the rod with pieces of timber and continue to work around it.
4 The completed pillar, one of a pair, is bonded to the wall and could be used as a support for a gate. For uniformity and a harmonious design, both the pillar and the wall have been rendered (pargeted) and then washed with diluted paint. While the wall was finished off with bricks laid on edge, brick pavers were used to top the pillars.

Left: *The completed piers blend well with both the brick wall and the path.*

Patios

A PATIO CAN EXTEND YOUR OUTDOOR LIVING SPACE AND PROVIDE YOU WITH A COMFORTABLE PLACE TO RELAX AND ENTERTAIN DURING SUMMER MONTHS. A PATIO IS NOT ONLY DURABLE AND PRACTICAL BUT IT WILL ALSO BE RELATIVELY EASY TO BUILD YOURSELF. LAYING A PATIO LIES WELL WITHIN THE CAPABILITIES OF ANY ENTHUSIASTIC HANDYMAN AND NEED NOT TAKE LONG TO COMPLETE.

PLANNING

Before planning your patio, try to get everyone who will use it to agree on what needs it should fulfil. Then you can decide on where, ideally, it should be sited, the features it should possess, its size, as well as other details.

SITE

There are usually several possibilities when it comes to siting a patio on any one property. It may lead off a living area of the house or may even be sited away from any buildings, perhaps alongside a pool or barbecue area. The decision will depend largely on the function your patio will fulfil although certain additional, yet basic, factors must be taken into account.

Will it, for instance, receive any sun; be sheltered from the midday sun and pro-

tected from the full force of the wind? If you are looking for a place where you can sit and read, try to make use of the shade from any existing trees when siting your patio, especially if they are growing in an unappealing, 'dead' area in your garden or backyard that is not being utilized. A paved area could transform such a spot into a pleasing and easily maintained retreat.

A patio to be used for frequent sunbathing should be exposed to the sun for most of the day, but if you intend to use the patio for dining or entertaining, it should offer both sun and some shade, as well as being accessible from the kitchen.

Right: *Mellow brick in a 'basketweave' pattern creates a traditional effect.*

Below: *A well-lit paving slab patio.*

SIZE

The patio should be built to a size that will serve your purpose for it. It is usually best to make it slightly larger than you think you would like it to be. If yours is a growing family, try and assess what your needs will be in years to come so that you are not forced to extend the patio later on.

For a patio which will be used for dining, there must be enough space to accommodate a table and sufficient chairs. When planning your patio area, leave enough room for a table and chairs, as well as any other furniture you may want to use. If space is at a premium, built-in furniture takes up much less space than

MATERIALS

You can use many different paving materials for a patio, including bricks, concrete paving blocks, stone 'flags' and concrete paving slabs. The range gives a choice of colours and of finishes, ranging from smooth (easy to clean, but potentially slippery) to a rough-hewn or 'riven' finish (safer to walk on, but more difficult to keep clean). You do not have to use only one material: interest can be created by mixing materials and colours.

PRINCIPLES

When it comes to building a sound and attractive patio, several important principles must be considered.
* The area to be paved must have a firm, well-compacted sub-base to avoid sagging and possibly even the eventual collapse of the paving.
* Proper drainage is essential to direct the flow of rainwater away from buildings and prevent unsightly puddles forming during rainy periods.
* All brick and block paving (but not slabs) should be contained within a sound framework to prevent it from breaking up at the edges over time.
* The paving should be laid flat with a slight slope for drainage. Protruding bricks, blocks or slabs not only look ugly; they can also be hazardous.
    With an appreciation of these priorities, you will be ready to consider the principles of patio-building in detail.

DRAINAGE

The very nature of outdoor patios and other paved areas makes drainage essential. Proper planning and thorough preparation will prevent puddles from forming whenever it rains.
    A patio should be built on a well-drained site that will dry out quickly after rain. The finished surface of a patio adjoining any building should be at least 150 mm (6 in) below the existing damp-proof course (vapor barrier). This is formed by inserting a strip of plastic sheeting or other impervious material into the brickwork of external walls just above ground level and below your final floor level to prevent damp from rising.
    The patio must slope away from the building at a gradient of 1-in-50 or a drop of 20 mm in every 1 m (1 in/4 ft), to prevent water from collecting at the base of the walls or in puddles on the patio itself.
    The paved area can be sloped towards its outer edge, to drain away naturally into a lawn or a large flower bed. In high rainfall areas, however, your lawn could become swampy, in which case rainwater must be channelled away, either to the road, a stormwater drain or simply into well-drained soil. It must not be

free-standing pieces. Seating can be built in to accommodate a movable table in a corner.
    If the patio adjoins the house, French or sliding doors often make access and movement between the two areas easier. In this way your patio could become a natural extension of your home.

SHAPE

Your patio's shape should complement existing features and buildings. If your flower beds follow gentle curves, try to design a patio that mirrors their flow, even if it does mean putting a little extra work into the paving.

STYLE AND FINISH

The way you design and furnish your patio will largely depend on the style of your house, but try to keep it simple. Too much colour and too many plant containers or pieces of movable furniture dotted about can sometimes create visual confusion and a cluttered effect. The key is to link together all aspects of the house and patio so that they blend harmoniously.
    If you are not a keen gardener, opt for a low-maintenance patio with hardy plants. There is no reason for the area to look dull: many shrubs, climbers, ground-covering plants and even trees that need little attention are available.

channelled to any drain leading to a sewer, septic tank or cesspool, but can be taken to a rainwater soakaway. A patio that is completely enclosed will certainly need a drainage channel or underground piping to lead off water.

EDGING

Brick or concrete paving blocks must be held in place by some sort of edging. However, where it is laid alongside existing structures – such as boundary walls or the sides of your house – edging may not be necessary as the structure will help contain the paving.

Where there are no abutting structures, an edging can be formed with a pre-cast concrete curbstone or by pouring concrete *in situ* around the perimeters of the paving. Alternatively, and more commonly, a brick or block edging may be laid. Bricks or blocks can be set end to end, against the paving, or lengthways at right angles to the paving, depending on the area to be contained. Either way, they should be set in mortar on a concrete strip foundation.

A free-standing brick or concrete block patio will have to be held in place by such an edging on all four sides in much the same way as a brick or concrete block drive (see page 55). Do not lay all the edgings first, however, as you could end up with an odd-shaped space which forces you to cut a number of bricks or blocks to make them fit. Instead, begin by laying your edging on one side only.

To lay the edging, use a builder's line to mark out the area, and dig an even, shallow trench around the outside. Lay a strip of concrete for a foundation and let it dry. Butter the bricks and lay them in the usual way (see page 89). Finish by forming a flaunching of mortar along the outside.

Patios made from stone flags or concrete paving slabs do not need a separate edging, though one could be added for visual effect if required. Bricks on edge make an interesting contrast.

Types of paving bond

Left (reading clockwise from top left):

Herringbone creates visual interest.

Basketweave (parquet) looks neat.

Staggered or half basketweave.

Stack bond is acceptable for paving but not for walls.

Bordered grid for a traditional effect.

Stretcher bond provides strength.

Preparation

Common sense indicates the importance of a solid foundation, especially if your patio is planned for a high traffic area or is to form the base for a carport. A solid, level and well-compacted sub-base is imperative. If necessary, get an expert's opinion on the type of soil you are planning to build on.

Soil with a high clay or peat content, making it unstable and highly water retentive, will often need a layer of hardcore, which consists of broken bricks, stones or other hard material. The depth of the hardcore will depend on the instability of the soil and on the use to which the patio is put, but it is usually 50 to 100 mm (2 to 4 in) deep for garden patios and 100 to 250 mm (4 to 10 in) for patios used regularly by vehicles.

The surface of the patio should end up at least 150 mm (6 in) below the damp-proof course (vapor barrier), and should have a slight slope for drainage. To work out the exact depth to which the soil needs to be excavated, add together the depths of the layer of hardcore (if used), the paving material, and the layer of sand on which they will sit.

The soil from a patio site must first be excavated to the right depth and the site levelled. Lighter-coloured subsoil should not be used for levelling – use hardcore instead. Well-compacted hardcore forms

Right: *Different and interesting effects can be created if paving slabs of varying sizes are used. Reconstituted concrete paving slabs, arranged in a neat pattern, have been used here.*

Edging patterns

Left (reading from left to right):

Bricks laid at an angle in concrete.

Curbstones positioned where the public road adjoins a brick driveway.

Curved soldier course edging.

the first layer, followed by a 25 to 50 mm (1 to 2 in) layer of fine concreting sand which can be compacted with a garden roller. Bricks and blocks can be laid directly on the sand (see *Driveways*, page 53 for details); paving slabs are put down on dabs of mortar.

TOOLS AND MATERIALS

Once you have planned the area to be paved, you can estimate the quantity of bricks required. A useful rule of thumb is to allow 45 clay bricks or blocks for every square metre (38 per sq yd). Concrete and clay bricks are both suitable and available in various colours. For 450 mm (18 in) square paving slabs, allow five per sq m (four per sq yd).

You will need hardcore for the base and cement, sand and aggregate for the foundations, for the edging and for holding slabs in place (see *Quantifying Materials* on page 87) and clean concreting sand for the paving base.

Your base surface must be firm and well-compacted before you start paving. You will need either a tamping or ramming tool, or a compacting machine

Left: *How to break a slab neatly.*

Below: *A brick patio provides a mellow setting for a colourful flower bed.*

(which may be hired in most large centres). For the various other tools required for paving, see page 80.

Step-by-step paving slab patio
To cover an area of 6 x 5 m (19 ft 8 in x 16 ft 5 in), you will need:

150 paving slabs 450 mm sq (18 in sq)
2,650 kg or 53 cu ft (5,830 lb) hardcore
2,100 kg or 53 cu ft (4,620 lb) fine concreting sand, for bedding

Mortar
Cement and sand mixed in the ratio 1:5
45 kg or 1 bag (110 lb) cement
225 kg or 5½ cu ft (495 lb) builder's sand

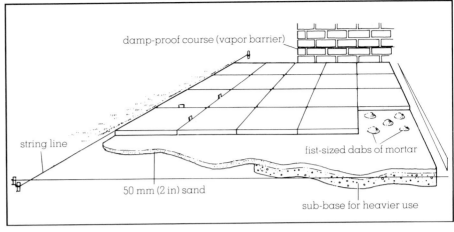

damp-proof course (vapor barrier)

string line

fist-sized dabs of mortar

50 mm (2 in) sand

sub-base for heavier use

1 Clear the site of all existing material (soil, vegetation etc) and excavate to an even depth of 150 to 350 mm (6 to 14 in) below the final level of the paving (depending on the thickness of the slabs and the depth of foundation required), ensuring the patio is at least 150 mm (6 in) below the house wall damp proof course (vapor barrier) and that it has a slope away from the building of 20 mm in each metre (1 in/4 ft).
2 Spread a layer of hardcore appropriate to the use (50 mm [2 in] for most patios; more for unstable soils or heavy use) and compact with a hand compactor – a heavy weight on the end of a pole. Spread 50 mm (2 in) of fine concreting sand on top of the hardcore and rake and roll this level.
3 To ensure accurate alignment of the paving slabs, mark out the area carefully with string and line pegs. To lay the first slab, put five fist-sized lumps of mortar on the sand and lower the slab into place. Use the handle of a club hammer to tap the slab into place, checking its position with a spirit level – in the direction of drainage, use a wooden off-cut under one end of the level to ensure the correct fall.
4 Subsequent slabs are laid, using the first as a guide, with thin (6 to 8 mm, ¼ in) plywood spacers between the slabs. As well as the five lumps of mortar, place a thin strip of mortar along the edge of the slabs already laid, which will form most of the finished mortar joint.
5 Check the level of each slab as it is laid and if too low or too high at any point, lift it and add or remove mortar.
6 Lay all the full-size slabs first. At the edges, you will need to cut or shape slabs to fit. Score a groove all around the slab with a wide-bladed cold chisel and club hammer and then tap the back of the slab with the club hammer until it breaks.
7 To finish off, remove all spacers after 24 hours and 'point' the joints with fresh mortar, making sure with a wooden or thin sheet material 'mask' that mortar does not get on to the face of the slab and is well pushed down into the joint.

hand compactor

hardcore

plywood spacer

groove

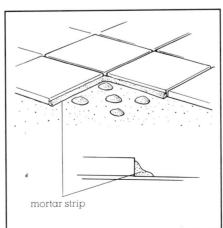

mortar strip

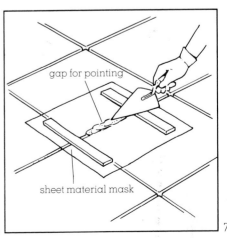

gap for pointing

sheet material mask

Paths

Strategically positioned, paths can provide convenient access and a firm surface between the house and other parts of the property or its boundary. They can follow a defined route from the garage or carport to the front door, from a swimming pool, clothes drying area or barbecue to the house, or simply lead to special features such as a pond, a herb garden or perhaps a bench. The pathway itself should be visually attractive but unobtrusive.

Location

Including a path in your outdoor design will usually be motivated by the simple need to link two or more areas, but sensitive planning is essential.

While the shortest route between points may frequently be indicated by a worn stretch of lawn, it may not be the best line to follow. Unless your setting is formal and symmetrically planted, try to avoid pathways which run straight down the middle of the lawn from entrance gate to front door, ruthlessly bisecting the space. Instead, consider curving the path to echo a line of flower beds. If necessary, move the gate to create a less rigid design. But beware of making paths *too* curved – the result could be that everyone takes a short cut across the grass!

A large site can often accommodate winding paths which lead to alluringly concealed corners and shielded features. If yours is a small site, however, a maze of little paths will simply make the area seem smaller.

Materials

Paths should generally be made of hard-wearing materials which are easy to maintain. For safety, the surfaces should be level and non-slip. Taking this into consideration, the most sensible materials to choose are brick, stone or concrete, either solid concrete or concrete blocks or slabs. Other possible materials include gravel (or pea shingle) and cobblestones. Materials can be used on their own or in combination. Railway sleepers (railroad ties) become slippery when wet, but strips of paving between the sleepers (ties) would solve this problem, and look attractive too. Laying paving bricks in between concrete paving blocks cuts down on material costs and creates interest at the same time. Otherwise, a sweet-smelling ground-covering plant like thyme or minty pennyroyal could be planted between bricks at intervals, to lend colour and aroma.

For best effect, a path must blend with the overall environment. Ideally, materials used should correspond with those used elsewhere in the garden – around a pool, on an existing patio or for any walls. Steps should also be constructed from the same material as any paths that extend from them.

Safety

As well as having a non-slip surface, it is important that paths are safe in other ways. Steps can be a particular hazard and should not be positioned where they might come as a surprise – just around a

Left: Stone chippings add visual appeal to these concrete paving slabs.

Left: *Concrete paving slabs neatly divide up the planted areas.*

corner, for example. Both steps and the main path surface should be kept clean (especially if moss or slime start to form) and kept clear of slippery leaves in the autumn. To make paths and steps safer at night, good lighting is essential – either overhead or at low level or built into a wall alongside the path.

WIDTH

Common sense will tell you how wide a pathway should be, as this will largely be dictated by its function. Its width should, though, be in proportion to the size of the surrounding site. To accommodate two people walking abreast, a path should theoretically be about 1.5 m (5 ft) wide. Few modern houses, however, have paths of such generous proportions. The brick pathway in our step-by-step project, which links a pool area with the patio, is 900 mm (3 ft) wide, which fits in well in a site of this size.

The height of the top of a path should be level with or slightly below the surrounding grassed areas so that a lawnmower can be used without damaging the paving (or the lawnmower blade!).

FOUNDATIONS

Paths do not normally need quite the same depth of foundations as either patios or drives. For most materials, a 50 mm (2 in) layer of sand is all that is required: on clay and peat soils, a hardcore sub-base may be needed.

EDGING

Solid concrete paths and paths made from concrete paving slabs do not need any edging, though a contrasting edging could be added for visual effect. All the other main materials (brick, concrete block, cobbles and gravel or pea shingle), however, do need some kind of edging to hold the material in place and prevent it from spreading.

This edging could be pre-cast concrete strips (or, for curved paths, plywood or flexible plastic). For a concrete block path, the blocks themselves can be used as an edging, mortared onto a concrete foundation.

When building a brick path, the most common method of laying an edging is to set the bricks in concrete – lengthways or end to end. Alternatively, a single row of bricks could be laid in an upright soldier course, or they may be set in a zig-zag course like a row of falling dominoes.

Left: *This curved brick path echoes the shape of the wall beside it.*

Paths

Preparation

The first step is to mark the outline of the path. Pegs and string lines can be used for a straight path; for a curved path, a hose or string can be adjusted to give different curves and will help you to visualize the end result at the planning stage.

It is quite feasible to lay a path on slightly sloping ground, but steps (see page 24) should be incorporated if the incline is too steep to use comfortably.

To make a path, the first task is to excavate the site to the required depth (50 mm [2 in] plus the depth of the paving material, allowing for any mortar needed) with a drainage crossfall of 1 in 40 (25 mm/m or 1½ in/5 ft). If required, the centre of the path could be the highest point with a gentle slope equally in either direction. With an otherwise flat path, there should ideally be a fall along the length (away from the house) of 1 in 100 (10 mm/m or 1 in/8 ft).

The sand sub-base (plus any hardcore if required) must be well compacted (hand compaction with a hand compactor or roller is enough for a garden path) before the paving material is laid.

Paths in different materials

You can choose any material you like for a garden path (and you may want to have more than one path, each in a different material), but the guideline should normally be that the material matches another material elsewhere in the site – either a patio area, a drive or the walls of the house itself.

Each material has its advantages and disadvantages and sometimes you may be able to compensate for these by combining one or more different materials in the same design.

Paving slabs
Pre-cast concrete paving slabs come in various sizes, shapes, colours and textures – for a path (especially a sloping path), the smoothest surfaces should obviously be avoided.

Least expensive are the plain square and rectangular designs, but these can be made to look more interesting and attractive by combining different sizes, colours and shapes.

Paving slabs can be laid directly on to sand or, preferably, on dabs of mortar on a hardcore sub-base (see *Patios*, page 43). Edging is unnecessary.

Gaps are left between paving slabs which can be filled with mortar at the end. This is done by brushing on a mixture of 1 part cement to 4 parts sand, making sure it goes down all the gaps and then hosing the surface off with water.

Paving slabs are not suitable for curved paths because of the amount of cutting and shaping involved.

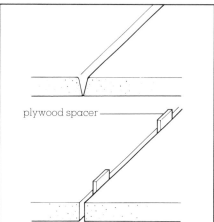

plywood spacer

Crazy paving
This uses broken slabs and looks less monotonous than regular designs. With crazy paving, time is needed to find a satisfactory pattern with minimum gaps and also to adjust the thickness of the sand below the paving since the slabs will often be of an unequal thickness.

No edging is needed. You may need to go over the gaps two or three times with dry mortar to fill them. Crazy paving can usually accommodate gentle curves.

Left: *Plywood spacers are used to hold the gaps between paving slabs until they are filled in with mortar.*

Left: *A concrete path is often best in a functional part of the garden.*

Stone

Flagstones are laid in a similar way to concrete paving slabs and crazy paving, but because stone is a natural material, it can look more attractive.

Granite sets (paving blocks)

Granite sets are commonly found on older city streets as a paving material, but can look effective in the home as well. You will need to excavate more deeply than with other materials as the sets are themselves thicker; sets are best laid on a mortar bed and the gaps filled with a dry mortar mix as for paving slabs.

No special edging is required, provided the outer rows of sets are put firmly in place first.

Bricks

Bricks can be used for paths, but may need to be frost-resistant. Special, thinner brick pavers can also be used.

The advantage of brick is that it has an attractive finish and can often match well with a brick house. On the other hand, it is a fairly expensive material and is time-consuming to lay. Bricks can either be laid on a bed of sand (see the step-by-step instructions in the next section) or on a 50 mm (2 in) layer of mortar. In either case, firm edging is required to retain the bricks in place.

Concrete blocks

Concrete blocks are generally thicker than concrete paving slabs and come in a range of different shapes, colours and textures. They are laid on a compacted bed of sand (see *Driveways*, page 53) and require a firm edging.

Gravel

Gravel is the name given to sharp edged chippings of crushed stone and the size

Below: *Using a mallet to level crazy paving slabs on a bed of sand.*

compacted sand base

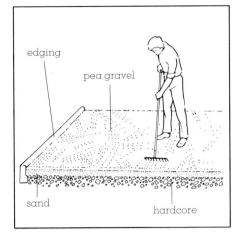

edging
pea gravel
sand
hardcore

Above: *Raking pea gravel evenly across a hardcore base.*

and colour depends on where it comes from. It can either be laid loose or bonded to an emulsion base which will stop it moving around.

Gravel is laid to a thickness of around 25 mm (1 in) over a hardcore sub-base blinded with sand (to fill in the gaps). It needs a stone, concrete, brick or timber edging to keep it in place, but even so will need frequent raking to keep an even spread plus occasional weedkilling. It is very suitable for use on curved paths, but not suitable for sloping ones.

Pea shingle is treated in the same way as gravel – it consists of small rounded stones sold in graded sizes.

Solid concrete

A solid concrete path can be inexpensive, but may look dull (and be slippery) unless it is textured by pressing stone chippings into the surface or by brushing as it sets to roughen the surface or to expose some of the aggregate. An unusual and attractive path can be created by adding coloured pigments to the concrete.

Although concrete does not need an edging, it does need formwork in order to lay it. For a garden path, a thickness of around 75 mm (3 in) is sufficient: it can be laid directly onto firm soil, though soft soil will need a hardcore base.

Solid concrete is particularly suitable for making a curved path; here, it will be best to hire flexible metal 'roadforms' to give the correct shape. For details of how to lay concrete, see *Working with Concrete*, page 91. For paths, you should use paving mix – 1 part cement, 1½ parts sand and 2½ parts aggregate – and put a joint in the path every 2 m (6 ft 6 in) or so.

Below: *Here a raised pond forms the focal point while brick paths lead off to other areas of interest and elegantly divide up the space.*

Paths

Cobbles

Cobbles are egg-shaped stones which can be used to create paved areas by laying them in a bed of mortar.

There are two ways to lay cobbles – on edge, where you want to *discourage* people from walking on a particular area or flat, where they are to be used as part of a path or other paved area.

Cobbles are commonly used to break up the monotony of other paving materials rather than on their own.

Paving in a lawn

To create a different effect, individual concrete slabs or stone flags can be laid as 'stepping stones' across a lawn surface. They do not need to be regular shapes – in fact, odd-shaped pieces are often best if the 'path' is to be curved.

To lay this type of paving, holes have to be made in the lawn to put in hardcore and the slabs or flags can then be laid on dabs of mortar so that the surface is flush with or just below the lawn surface. Use the slab itself as a guide for cutting through the turf and then dig carefully to keep the sides of the hole vertical.

Above right: *Using a tamping beam to tamp cobbles into a dry mortar mix.*

Right: *Laying individual paving slab 'stepping stones' in a lawn.*

dry mortar mix

tamping beam

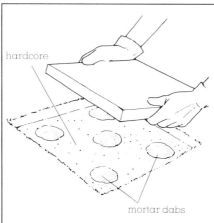

hardcore

mortar dabs

Step-by-step curved brick path

You will need normal bricklaying tools for constructing the edging and a rubber mallet for firming the bricks into place (or a club hammer used on top of a piece of timber). For a path 6 m (22 ft 2 in) long and 0.9 m (3 ft) wide, following our method, you will also need:

Edging foundation

Concrete mix 1:2½:3½ (cement:sand: aggregate) and 1:2:6 (cement:lime:sand) for mortar
50 kg (110 lb) bag of cement
70 kg or 2 cu ft (154 lb) sand
110 kg or 2¼ cu ft (242 lb) aggregate
60 kg or 1½ cu ft (132 lb) builder's sand
8 kg (18 lb) lime
OR 16 ml (½ fl oz) plasticizer
Black polythene sheet (optional)

Brickwork

240 paving bricks
235 kg or 6 cu ft (517 lb) concreting sand

1 First peg out your path and lay string or a hose along the perimeters of the area to be paved. Demarcate the width with loosely laid paving bricks. Excavate to accommodate one brick depth and a 50 mm (2 in) layer of sand, removing all grass and vegetation. To accommodate a stretcher bond pattern, which is the pattern used here, two bricks in each alternate course will have to be cut prior to laying the paving bricks.

2 Level and compact the excavated site and lay plastic sheeting over the whole area to be paved. Lay a concrete foundation – about 200 mm wide and 40 mm deep (8 x 1½ in) – along the outer perimeters. Leave it to dry. Using the mortar mix, lay bricks along the edge, taking care to maintain an equal distance at all points, exactly the width of four bricks and to give a fall of around 20 mm (¾ in) across the path.

3 Fill in the area between the edgings with sand to just above the base of the paving bricks already laid. Smooth the sand with a shaped screeding board. Now press the bricks into the sand without mortar joints. Tap them gently with a rubber mallet to level them. If a brick is lower than it should be, pack a little extra sand under it. When all the bricks are snugly in position, sweep a dry cement: sand mixture (1:4) over the path and gently hose down so that all gaps are filled with mortar.

4 An attractive, curved brick path now connects the patio with the barbecue and pool area. The paving design used was stretcher bond, chosen to match both the new patio and other existing brickwork. Notice that all the extraneous black plastic sheeting along the outer edges of the path has been trimmed close to the brickwork with a utility knife. The re-established grass forms a lush green outline for the red brick.

3

2

4

PATHS

Step-by-step concrete path

A concrete path is laid very much in the same way as a concrete slab, except that it is longer and thinner and you may well want to make it curved.

Use paving mix concrete (1 part cement: 1½ parts sand: 2½ parts aggregate) laid 75 mm (3 in) thick with joints every 2 m (6½ ft) along the path. A sub-base will not normally be needed except on clay or peaty soil, but one can be used to build up levels if the top soil is thick (excavation should go down to subsoil level). The quantities of concrete and hardcore required for your path will depend on its width and length.

A curved path is likely to be more suit-able for most outdoor settings – curves can be made in the formwork either by using metal 'roadforms' or by notching (kerfing) the wood on the inside face forming the curve. For really sharp bends, use hard-board strips secured firmly in place.

The curved concrete path shown here was built in sections with expansion joints between each section. We take up the story as the last section is being laid.

1 A thin layer of hardcore was used as a sub-base 'blinded' with sand between straight and curved formwork.
2 Walking on the sand is sufficient to compact it and the hardcore.
3 Paving mix concrete is shovelled in between the forms making sure it gets right into the bottom corners.
4 A home-made hand compactor is sufficient to compact the first layer of concrete.
5 The space between the forms is slightly overfilled and compacted with a sawing motion of a home-made wooden tamping beam.
6 Extra aggregate is then sprinkled on to the surface and pushed in with a float.
7 A stiff brush and water spray exposes the aggregate to give an attractive and safe finish.

Right: *The completed concrete path is durable and provides a useful walkway.*

5

6

7

DRIVEWAYS

A SOLID CONCRETE, BRICK OR CONCRETE PAVING BLOCK DRIVEWAY NOT ONLY MAKES A GOOD FIRST IMPRESSION BUT ALSO PROVIDES A SURFACE ON WHICH YOU CAN PARK A CAR OR VAN.

OF ALL THE PAVED SURFACES AROUND THE HOME, THE DRIVEWAY IS THE ONE WHICH NEEDS TO BE ESPECIALLY WELL CONSTRUCTED WITH PROPER FOUNDATIONS. IF IT IS NOT, THE NEW SURFACE WILL SOON GET UNEVEN OR CRACKED AND WILL LOOK UNSIGHTLY.

ALTHOUGH IT IS HARD WORK, LAYING A NEW DRIVE IS A JOB WELL WITHIN THE CAPABILITIES OF AN ENTHUSIASTIC HANDYMAN (PREFER-ABLY WITH AN EQUALLY ENTHUSIASTIC HELPER), THOUGH SOME SPE-CIALIZED EQUIPMENT WILL NEED TO BE HIRED: A CONCRETE MIXER FOR SOLID CONCRETE DRIVES AND A PLATE VIBRATOR AND BLOCK SPLIT-TER (MASONRY SAW) FOR CONCRETE BLOCK DRIVES.

PLANNING

Although the siting of a driveway will usually be fairly obvious (typically between the road and the garage or leading to the front of the house if there is no garage), there are several points to bear in mind when considering the size and the exact location.

For a start, the drive must be wide enough so that the car doors can be opened on either side with enough room for people to get in and out and, if between garage and road, long enough so that the garage doors can be opened and the front gates closed with the car in position. The drive should not slope so much that the car will 'bottom' as it moves from

Above: *The unusual herringbone pattern of the walls is repeated in the drive.*

Left: *An original circular brick pattern has been used for this driveway.*

the garage to the drive or from the drive to the road.

For a drive in front of the house, you will want to ensure that parked cars do not obscure natural daylight and do not obstruct access to the house. The drive should not be so near to the house that the walls can be stained by exhaust fumes and should not be too close to the neighbouring houses.

MATERIALS

There is a wide choice of materials for constructing front drives.

Solid concrete is hard-wearing when properly laid and can be attractive if given a textured finish. Concrete is, however, susceptible to oil stains and although inexpensive is not easy to lay properly, especially on a slope. For information on how to lay a concrete slab, see page 92: a concrete drive needs to be at least 100 mm (4 in) thick or 150 mm (6 in) if on clay or other soft soil.

Concrete paving blocks give the strength of concrete but can be arranged in a much more attractive pattern. They can be laid in rectangular or interlocking 'shaped' patterns (see the diagram on the next page): they are laid on a compacted layer of sand with 100 mm (4 in) of crushed stone as the sub-base. Fine sand is then brushed on to the surface and compacted so that it 'locks' the blocks together by getting into the joints. No cement or mortar is needed, but the blocks must be positioned between firm edgings to keep them in place.

The most common size of concrete block is 200 mm (8 in) long, 100 mm (4 in) wide and 65 mm (2½ in) thick. The four common laying patterns are stretcher bond (similar to that used for a brick wall), parquet (basketweave), 45° herringbone and 90° herringbone.

The two herringbone patterns are good choices for a drive as they give a very strong bond.

Asphalt is often used for drives because it resists oil spills. However, it can be expensive to lay and is a job best left to a specialist contractor.

Concrete paving slabs can be used to construct a drive, but the necessary 'hydraulically-pressed' type and the deep foundations needed make laying a paving slab drive difficult and expensive (see *Patios* page 43 for details on how to lay concrete slab paving).

Bricks can be used for constructing drives as they are quite strong (especially

DRIVEWAYS

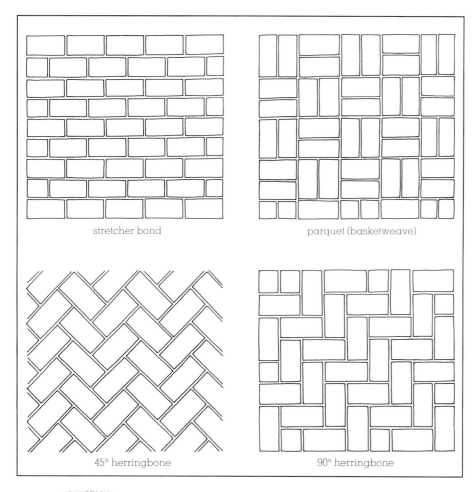

stretcher bond

parquet (basketweave)

45° herringbone

90° herringbone

Right: *The edge blocks of a drive are held in place with mortar.*

if laid on edge) but they may have to be the frost-free type. They can be laid on mortar, but need proper foundations.

Gravel is an attractive and inexpensive material for a drive and easy to maintain as you simply shovel on more gravel. It also copes well with oil spills, but in time can become untidy. Gravel is best used with other materials – perhaps as an oil trap in a paved or concreted area.

PRINCIPLES

Installing a drive means following some important constructional principles.
* The area to be paved must have a firm, well-compacted base to prevent the paving from sagging and/or cracking.
* The drive surface must have a slope to carry rainwater away across and, preferably, along the surface. If the drive slopes towards the house or garage, a drainage channel must be incorporated.
* Drives which are constructed from bricks or blocks must have proper edging restraint to prevent them from breaking up at the edges.

If these principles are not followed, the drive will look unsightly and will be damaged by the weight of vehicles on it.

FOUNDATIONS

Most drives need a foundation of at least 100 mm (4 in) of crushed stone, quarry waste or 'hoggin' (clayey gravel) – do not use normal hardcore. The sub-base must be well-compacted. For concrete block drives, this is covered with a 65 mm (2½ in) layer of fine concreting sand which is compacted down to 50 mm (2 in).

DRAINAGE

The minimum drainage crossfall for a drive is 1 in 40 (25 mm/m or 3 in/10 ft). If you do not ensure a proper slope, water will collect and may damage the house walls. If possible, there should also be a fall of 1 in 100 (10 mm/m or 1 in/8 ft).

The rainwater needs to be disposed of properly. For a large drive draining into the garden or a drive sloping back towards the garage, you will need to incorporate drainage channels to collect it, connected to underground drainage pipes to take it to a soakaway or storm drain – not to a drain leading to a sewer, cesspool or septic tank.

Drainage channels can be pre-cast concrete, fibre-cement sections, *in situ* concrete, bricks or plastic with a metal grid on top.

Left: *A complicated but rewarding pattern known as 'hopsack'.*

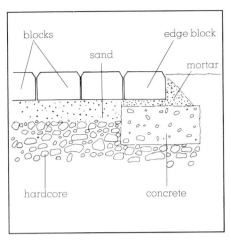

EDGING

When making a brick or concrete block drive, a firm edging, mortared in place, must be provided to prevent the bricks at the sides from cracking or falling out. The edging can be the same material as the drive, or pre-cast concrete edging strip can be used. Either way, it needs to be installed with the correct drainage fall and is put in before the main paving material – which makes calculating the exact size of the drive crucial.

Below: *A brick drive in herringbone.*

SITE PREPARATION

All soil, vegetation (including tree roots) and old drive materials must be removed from the site. For concrete drives, the depth of excavation will need to be 200 to 250 mm (8 to 10 in) below the final finished surface; for concrete block drives around 215 mm (8½ in).

Make sure that the base of the hole has the correct drainage fall from the start so that an even layer of sub-base material can be put down.

TOOLS AND EQUIPMENT

The tools needed for constructing a concrete drive are the same as those needed for laying a concrete slab (see page 92); a compacting machine would be useful for the sub-base.

For a concrete block drive, you will need normal bricklaying tools, but here a plate vibrator and a block splitter (masonry saw) are essential pieces of equipment which you will be able to hire from most major building centres.

Below: *Using a plate vibrator to compact paving slabs.*

Bottom: *It is important to protect the finished paving while using a block splitter.*

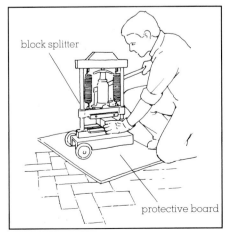

Driveways

Step-by-step concrete block drive
For a drive 4 m (13 ft) by 8 m (26 ft), you will need 1600 paving blocks (100 x 200 x 65 mm [4 x 8 x 2½ in]) and:

Sub-base/foundation
5½ tonnes or 110 cu ft (5½ tons) of hoggin, Type 1 base material or similar
3 tonnes or 70 cu ft (3 tons) of sand
67 kg or 1⅓ bags (145 lb) cement
170 kg or 4¼ cu ft (375 lb) concreting sand
280 kg or 5½ cu ft (620 lb) aggregate

Mortar
25 kg or ½ bag (55 lb) cement
110 kg or 3 cu ft (240 lb) builder's sand
13 kg (28 lb) lime
OR 25 ml (1 fl oz) plasticizer

1 Dig out the foundations first, taking care not to disturb any underground pipes or cables. Distribute top soil elsewhere in the garden, but dispose of subsoil and old drive materials. Dig out to the required depth with the correct slope and tamp the soil down firmly with a hand compactor – a large weight on a pole (also known as a punner).
2 Shovel in the hoggin or crushed stone to a depth of at least 100 mm (4 in), raking it out so that it is level.
3 The plate vibrator is then used to compact the sub-base.
4 The next stage is to install the edging blocks which are mortared in place onto concrete 75 to 100 mm (3 to 4 in) deep: careful measurement is necessary to ensure the edging blocks are correctly spaced to take the block pattern between them using an exact number of block widths and also to make sure that they are laid to the correct fall either across or along the drive. A good 'fillet' of mortar should be placed outside the edging blocks so that it will hold them in place. Let the mortar set before moving on to the next stage.
5 The sub-base should be 115 mm (4½ in) below the level of the edging. To estimate the thickness of sand you need, lay a small area 65 mm (2½ in) deep, place some concrete blocks on it and compact them with a piece of timber and a hammer. They should come down to just above the edge restraint. Work out whether you need slightly more or slightly less than this for the whole site and then make up a shaped screeding board which you can use to get the correct thickness. Rake the sand roughly before using the screeding board.
6 The blocks are laid, starting at the bottom of a slope or from one edge. Lay the blocks on the sand base, sliding them down the side of the blocks already

---

Right: *The completed drive has been neatly finished off at the edges and around the central drain.*

in place so that they fit snugly together. Where you are laying a pattern which means that full blocks will not fit at the edges, leave a gap and continue. Always work from the previously laid blocks (kneel on a board) and never from the sand.

The edge blocks can be cut to shape with a hammer and a wide-bladed cold chisel, but it is easier and more accurate to use a block splitter (masonry saw) – mark a chalk line on the block where you want to cut it, put it in the splitter and cut it. Lay all the edging blocks until the whole surface is covered (or for very large areas, until you have done around 10 sq m or 100 sq ft).

Use the plate vibrator to lower the surface of the blocks. It does this by compacting the sand layer and, at the same time, levelling the blocks and forcing some sand up into the joints to hold them secure. If vibrating a partly laid drive, stay at least 1 m (3 ft 3 in) away from the laying face or the blocks will be disturbed. Two or three passes are usually necessary to get the blocks to the correct height; if any blocks crack during this process, replace them with new ones. Finish off the rest of the drive if necessary and vibrate that.

7 The final stage is to brush fine joint-filling sand over the whole drive and make two more passes with the plate vibrator to force this down into the joints.

6

7

Walls

Traditionally, walls were built to define boundaries as well as to act as a defence against animals and other intruders. While security is still a major motivation for many people, the building of walls on urban properties is increasingly influenced by a need for privacy and protection from noise and unsightly views. But as well as being functional, walls can be aesthetically pleasing and attractive features in their own right.

Boundary walls

The extent of the average boundary wall may be enough to daunt even an ardent do-it-yourselfer initially. Plan it logically, tackle it at your own pace, and you will find that it is not such an impossible task after all. For novice wall builders, the place to start is with low walls – perhaps retaining walls, dividing walls and screens – and to move on to higher boundary walls and walls on slopes when the basic techniques have been mastered.

When planning a wall around your property, make sure that you identify the exact boundary line and build within it, ensuring that the foundations do not extend beyond the line. If you are having a new house built, boundary walls should ideally be part of the initial construction. This way it may also be possible to finance the work from your mortgage (bond), thus saving capital outlay later. Suitable materials for boundary and other types of walls are as follows:

Bricks come in a wide range of different colours, textures and shapes. For outside use, you need ordinary-quality *facing* bricks – special-quality bricks are needed only for sites subject to severe frost or extreme weather conditions.

Below: *A low dividing wall incorporating planters and protruding headers.*

Natural stone can be expensive and difficult to obtain as a wall-building material. Although one of the most attractive of materials, it can be difficult to work with if the sizes are very uneven and, for most do-it-yourselfers, reconstituted stone is a more practical choice.

Concrete blocks used for outside walling generally have textured faces with an aggregate of crushed natural stone built into them – hence the term 'reconstituted stone'. The blocks can come in clay brick-sized lumps, as 'multistones' (the size of several bricks with imitation mortar courses already built in) or as random sizes to simulate the effect of building a natural stone wall.

Above: *An ambitious boundary wall in reconstituted stone.*

Screen blocks are also concrete but have a smooth face. They are pierced with an open pattern and can be used on their own to build a wall or with solid bricks or concrete blocks as decoration. Screen blocks are more suitable for decorative, rather than strictly functional, walls.

Right: *Walls do not have to be straight and flat. Here the planters and the gaps between the bricks create interesting and unusual effects.*

DIVIDING WALLS

Walls can be used to create interesting visual breaks outside – between patio and lawn, for example, or along the edges of a path or drive. Even low walls can be used to make a site more interesting, especially on a site which otherwise has no distinguishing features.

Higher walls can be built as a windbreak, to screen off certain areas (the compost heap, garbage area or vegetable patch, for example), or to create a private area. To reduce the cost, and to avoid completely hiding the area beyond the walls, screen walls can be made from pierced screen concrete blocks or with 'open bond' brickwork, both of which will let in light and air.

RETAINING WALLS

A retaining wall is used to hold back the soil where a sloping site has been terraced or where there is a difference in level between two parts of the site.

Retaining walls are not difficult to build, but care needs to be taken in choosing the correct materials and in the detailed design.

Left: *A reconstituted stone wall forms the perfect backdrop to this pond.*

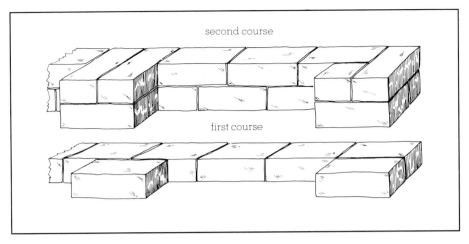

second course

first course

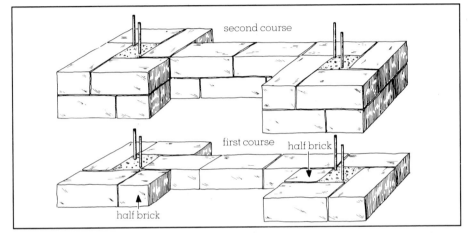

second course

first course · half brick

half brick

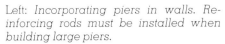

Left: *Incorporating piers in walls. Reinforcing rods must be installed when building large piers.*

675 mm (2 ft 3 in) if piers of at least twice the wall thickness are incorporated no more than 3 m (9 ft 9 in) apart. A one-brick wall 215 mm (8½ in) thick can go up to 1.35 m (4 ft 5 in) high without piers, but with piers of at least twice the wall thickness spaced no more than 3 m (9 ft 9 in) apart, the maximum height goes up to 1.8 m (6 ft).

Piers are built at the ends of the wall, at regular, intermediate points and where additional strength is required – for supporting a gate, for instance. When planning a wall which requires supporting piers, measure out the distance the wall will cover and plot the area where each pier will be built, so that you can lay a slightly wider foundation at these points to accommodate each one.

Building a pier is much the same as building a pillar (see page 34) and reinforcing rods should be provided where necessary. It should also be bonded in a similar manner to a pillar (see diagrams on page 37 for examples of three-brick and four-brick pillars). The opening is then cast full of mortar when the piers are completed (see diagram). When building a very large pillar or pier, or one that would have to bear load, concrete can be

Structural walls

Building the walls which go to make up a house is not a job for most experienced do-it-yourself enthusiasts. But low walls for a conservatory or garden building are no more difficult than any other type of outside wall, provided a damp-proof course (dpc or vapor barrier) is included in the construction (if necessary tying up with the house dpc) and the design of the wall meets any local planning or building legislation.

Height and width

First evaluate your needs carefully. For boundary walls, 1.8 m (6 ft) is a safe and suitable height from more than one point of view. It would be difficult for the average person to see or climb over such a wall, and it is around the maximum height to which a one- (or full-) brick wall (see our step-by-step project on pages 65 and 66) should be built, according to the local planning/building regulations in many areas. It may be a good idea to consult your local planning authority.

If this height is not adequate for your needs, bear in mind that wider and deeper foundations, expansion joints,

Left: *Concrete block walling can blend in well with concrete block paving.*

supporting pillars and, in some cases, brick reinforcement will be necessary.

Walls below 1.8 m (6 ft) will, however, need supporting piers, depending on their height and their thickness. For instance, a half-brick wall 102.5 mm (4 in) thick (sometimes called a single-brick wall as it is the thickness of one brick) can be built to a height of 450 mm (1 ft 6 in) without piers (except at the ends) or up to

Right: *Free-standing walls need supporting piers at regular intervals.*

Below: *Two half-brick walls built close together to act as a planter.*

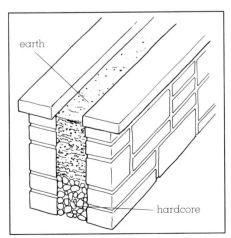

earth

hardcore

Walls

used instead of mortar for extra strength.

For added effect, two half-brick walls can be built alongside one another and the space in between filled with hardcore and then earth to act as a planter. Drain holes need to be made as with a retaining wall; for added strength, galvanized wall ties should be used at intervals to hold the two walls together.

Expansion joints

It is essential to provide expansion joints (a vertical joint that extends to the full height of the wall) to allow horizontal movement in walls. They should be provided at least every 6 m (19 ft 8 in) in

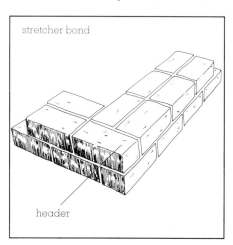

stretcher bond

header

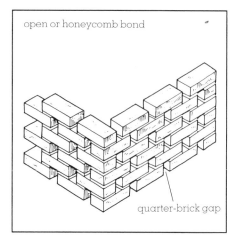

open or honeycomb bond

quarter-brick gap

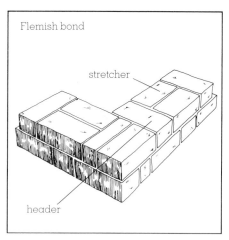

Flemish bond

stretcher

header

walls. The easiest place to incorporate an expansion joint is at a pier.

Bonds

There are a variety of bonds, all of which stagger joints in particular ways, producing different patterns when bricks or blocks are laid. While the visual effect will of course vary according to the bond chosen for construction, the practical reason for bonding the bricks or blocks is to tie them together in a solid mass. An unbonded wall would have vertical joints in straight lines, which would not distribute the load evenly along the length of the wall. It could even result in the eventual collapse of the wall.

Stretcher bond is the most commonly used bond and has bricks overlapping each other by half their length. Bricks are laid lengthways along a double or single line. In a half-brick wall, half bricks must be laid at the beginning and end of every second course to allow for bonding. In a one-brick wall, the end bricks may be laid across the two lines of brick.

Open or honeycomb bond is a decorative form of stretcher bond with quarter- or half-brick spaces between the ends of each brick. It looks attractive and cuts

Left and below: The different types of bond produce various patterns.

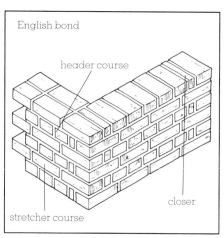

English bond

header course

stretcher course

closer

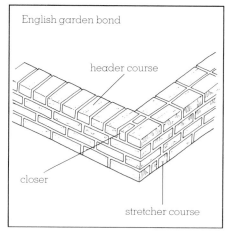

English garden bond

header course

closer

stretcher course

down on the number of bricks required to build a wall, thus saving money.

Flemish bond is used for one-brick walls and consists of headers and stretchers in the same course. To stagger the joints at the corners, it is necessary to incorporate closers (bricks cut in half lengthways) in alternate courses.

Flemish garden wall bond is similar to ordinary Flemish bond, but has two or three stretchers followed by a header in every course. Once again, closers must be used to aid bonding.

English bond is formed by alternating courses of headers and stretchers so avoiding a vertical joint in the centre of the wall. Some say this is the strongest bond, so it is often used for retaining walls. Closers are used to stagger the joints in the header course.

English garden wall bond is formed by laying three courses of ordinary stretcher bond followed by one header course. Once again closers should be used to stagger the joints.

Joints

When building walls and other features of brick, it is necessary to neaten and shape the joints between bricks. This process, also known as pointing, usually takes place when the mortar is still wet. A variety of pointing tools may be used (see *Tools*, page 80), or you can cut a piece of

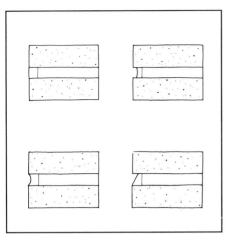

Above: *The diagram shows the four main types of joint. They are (reading clockwise from top left): flush, recessed, weather struck and concave.*

metal and use it to rake out the joints.

Flush joints are quite literally flush with the brickwork. They may be formed by scraping off excess mortar with a small pointing trowel and then wiping clean the brickwork with sacking.

Weather struck joints are made by using a pointing trowel to form an angled recess in the mortar. This angle must slope downwards towards the outer surface of the wall, to allow rain to wash off. Vertical joints can slope to the left or right – but must all be the same!

Concave joints ('bucket-handle') are formed by smoothing the mortar with a pointing tool, a round jointer or a piece of reinforcing metal.

Recessed joints have a section raked out with a piece of wood or metal but, because they do not shed water well, are generally used only inside the house.

F<small>OUNDATIONS</small>

Low (less than 600 mm or 2 ft) half-brick walls can be built on top of paving slabs which have been laid on a full bed of mortar. But for strength and stability (especially on clay or peaty soils), all garden walls should be built on proper strip foundations.

The normal recommendation for half-brick walls up to 1 m (3 ft 3 in) is a concrete strip 100 to 150 mm (4 to 6 in) deep and 300 mm (12 in) wide. For one-brick walls up to 1 m (3 ft 3 in) high, the thickness

Above right: *The first step with foundations above ground is the formwork.*

Right: *Concrete is poured into the formwork and then levelled.*

Left: *To create a strip foundation for a wall, a trench must first be dug out of the ground.*

increases to 225 to 300 mm (9 to 12 in) and the width to 450 mm (18 in). For higher one-brick walls up to 1.8 m (6 ft), the depth should always be 375 to 450 mm (15 to 18 in) and the width 450 to 600 mm (18 in to 2 ft).

To save expense, well-compacted hardcore can be put in the trench first with concrete used to make up the total thickness. The depth of the trench should be 75 or 150 mm (3 or 6 in) more than the depth of the foundations so that the first one or two courses of the wall are below ground level. On very damp ground, you could use engineering bricks for these. The one-brick wall built for our step-by-step project is just over 800 mm (2 ft 8 in) high. A 110 mm deep x 400 mm wide (4¼ x 16 in) strip foundation was therefore quite adequate.

If you are unsure about your site, consult a surveyor or your local building inspector for advice.

CONSTRUCTION

Once you have decided where to site the wall, mark out the area along which it will extend, using pegs and a builder's line or string. The following measurements are based on the foundation built for our wall project; adapt them as required.

Remove all vegetation. Excavate a trench approximately 170 mm (6¾ in)

deep. Knock in the first peg at the lower end so that it protrudes 110 mm (4¼ in) from the trench bottom. Use a straight-edge with a level on top to bring the other pegs to the same level. On sloping ground steps need to be formed in the foundation strip. The height difference in the steps is equal to one or more courses of brick, depending on the steepness of the slope. The length of each step should be equal to the whole number of bricks. Use plywood off-cuts to retain the concrete in the step shapes until it sets. Overlap the steps by about 100 mm (4 in) so that they form continuously bonded structures; otherwise the steps could separate if there is any ground movement. Use a gauge rod to insert the pegs of the next level. Now wet the trench and pour in concrete up to the top of each peg. Leave it for 24 hours to dry.

TOOLS

Tools required will include most of those in your basic toolkit, the most important items being your spirit level, builder's square and, of course, a trowel. In addition, you will need a gauge rod and corner blocks, both of which are simple to make (see page 80); pegs and a builder's line (or string) as well as jointing tools. A tingle (see page 82), which can also be homemade from a scrap of metal or thin plywood, is very handy for keeping your

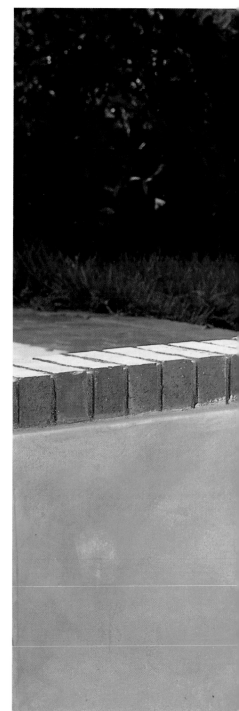

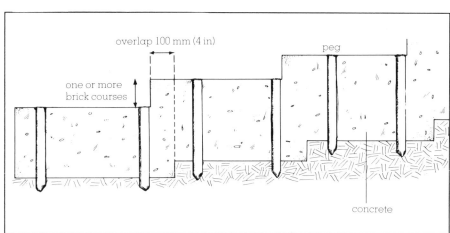

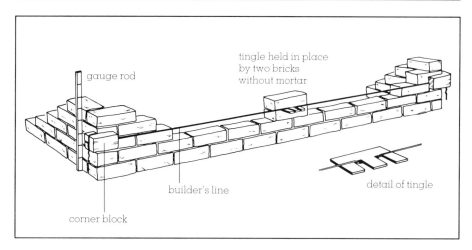

builder's line level over considerable distances.

You will also need a brick hammer (ax) or club hammer and bolster (brick set). If you anticipate cutting a large number of bricks, it would be a good idea to use an angle grinder.

Above left: *This profile shows how, on a sloping site, the trench foundation has been formed into steps, each of which is equal to one or more brick courses.*

Left: *Corner blocks and a tingle ensure that the wall is straight and that the courses are level.*

Materials

Once you have established the required length, width and height of your wall, it will be an easy exercise to determine how many bricks should be ordered. Remember that 55–60 bricks will be required for one square metre (45–50 a square yard) of half-brick walling, not including piers.

You will need cement, sand and aggregate for the foundation, as well as cement, lime (or plasticizer) and sand to mix mortar for laying the bricks.

Decide on how you wish to finish off the wall – rendering (pargeting) and painting is very effective and attractive.

Above: Although rendered (pargeted) and painted, the wall has a brick coping which maintains the brickwork theme.

Step-by-step one-brick wall

To build a 2 m (6 ft 6 in) long, 820 mm (2 ft 8 in) high, solid one-brick wall, with a foundation 2,200 mm × 400 mm (7 ft 3 in × 16 in) and 110 mm (4¼ in) deep, the materials you will need are:

Foundation

Concrete – 1:2½:3½ cement:sand:aggregate
25 kg or just over ½ x 100 lb bag cement
65 kg or 1¾ cu ft (143 lb) sand

100 kg or 2 cu ft (220 lb) aggregate

Brickwork

Height: 700 mm (2 ft 3 in) excluding 120 mm (4¾ in) facing brick coping
160 bricks
24 facing bricks (for coping)
38 kg (84 lb) cement
228 kg or 5¾ cu ft (503 lb) builder's sand
13 kg (29 lb) lime
OR 25 ml (1 fl oz) plasticizer

Render

16 kg (35 lb) cement
96 kg or 2½ cu ft (212 lb) builder's sand
8 kg (18 lb) lime
OR 16 ml (½ fl oz) plasticizer

WALLS

1 Using wooden pegs and a builder's line or string, mark out the planned area for your wall. Excavate a trench as described. Lay the strip foundation and leave to dry.

2 When the foundation has dried hard, set out your first course of bricks, without mortar, to ensure they will fit. Then lay them with mortar, checking carefully to make sure that they are square, level and plumb.

3 As your levels are crucial, continually check vertical and horizontal planes with a spirit level. Lightly tap bricks down with a trowel handle if necessary.

4 When building your end pier, ensure that the corners are at an angle of 90° with the use of a builder's square.

5 For a neat and efficient job, it is important to clean off excess mortar as you work, scraping the trowel upwards against the brick.

6 Although you are buttering the end of each brick as you go, it will be necessary to add mortar between the joints with a trowel.

7 With the gauge rod, continually check that the courses (and mortar joints) are even and regular. Rake out or point the joints with a metal scraper or trowel.

Continue laying brick courses until the full height of the wall is reached. In this project we have also rendered (pargeted) and painted the wall and added a brick coping.

4

6

5

7

RETAINING WALLS

Retaining walls usually support earth on sloping sites or where one plot is higher than the next. The weight of the soil increases as water collects behind the wall, and earth-retaining walls therefore have to be considerably more solid than free-standing walls. It also follows that the drainage of a retaining wall is of the utmost importance.

FUNCTION

On a steeply sloping site, a high retaining wall could be used in the creation of a single terrace offering a good view. Unless you are creating a patio, gradually sloping land is probably more appropriately moulded into several shallow terraces.

A retaining wall can often fulfil a dual purpose, by forming the backdrop to a waterfall or the back wall of a structure, such as a barbecue or a summerhouse. A flat, uninspiring site can be improved by a raised or terraced lawn, or a stylish sunken patio. As a border for a raised flower bed, a low retaining wall (not more than 600 mm [2 ft] high) can be finished or topped with paving bricks or wood and used as seating. A different effect can be created by covering a retaining wall with creepers or climbers, thus turning it into an attractive feature.

Above: A brick retaining wall used to enclose a flourishing flower bed.

DRAINAGE

If the earth behind a retaining wall were to become waterlogged, the whole structure could collapse, with disastrous consequences. Drainage is therefore a critical factor when building a sound retaining wall.

To ensure proper drainage, it is essential to leave adequate weepholes or to install drainage pipes at regular intervals along the base of the wall, thus preventing the accumulation of water behind the wall. Weepholes may be created by leaving quarter-brick gaps in the wall or by inserting a PVC drainage pipe, which is at least 40 mm (1½ in) in diameter.

For major walls or wet areas, it is wise to build a soakaway (see diagram). The space between the wall and the bank of earth is filled with hardcore, consisting of rubble, broken bricks, stones and gravel with the large aggregate towards the bottom. Lengths of PVC drainage pipe, at least 40 mm (1½ in) in diameter, should be inserted at regular intervals in the lowest course above ground level.

If a great deal of water drains through the pipe, it should drain away into a gutter or channel at the base of the wall.

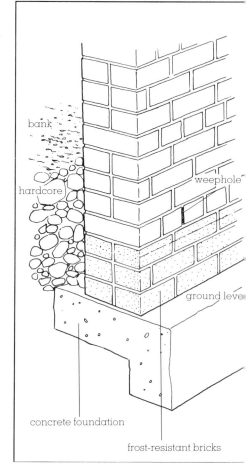

bank

hardcore

weephole

ground level

concrete foundation

frost-resistant bricks

Above: *This retaining wall cleverly matches the elegant flight of steps.*

MATERIALS

It is essential that your retaining wall is strong and solid enough to withstand the lateral pressure of soil and rainwater that it will have to bear. The strength of the wall lies in the foundation bonding and the mortar mix. Tough bonds which work well for retaining walls are the Flemish, English and English garden wall bond (see bonds, page 62).

Facing bricks are suitable for building a retaining wall, as they are strong and durable, though bricks below ground level should be frost-resistant or engineering bricks. For a smallish wall, such as the retaining wall in our step-by-step project, ordinary bricks would be adequate, provided they are rendered (pargeted). A wall which does not have to bear a considerable load may also be built using stretcher bond.

Left: *Here a quarter-brick gap has been left between two bricks to provide a weephole for drainage.*

Right: *A simple soakaway behind a retaining wall will ensure that excess rainwater drains away.*

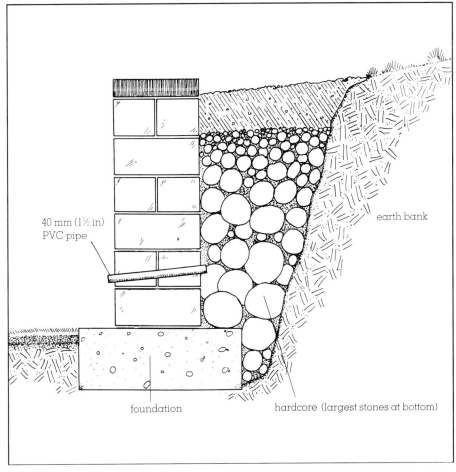

40 mm (1½ in) PVC pipe

earth bank

foundation

hardcore (largest stones at bottom)

WALLS

CONSTRUCTION

A retaining wall has to be much more solid than the average wall and its load-bearing capacity should be in proportion to the amount of earth it will have to retain.

Try also to keep your retaining wall proportionate to the scale of your garden or backyard – it should not dominate. If the slope is quite steep, it would be better, if possible, to make use of terraces, rather than build one high retaining wall. They will also be stronger, as a result, since each wall will carry less weight.

The higher and steeper the slope you plan to retain, the more critical the construction work will be. Foundations will certainly have to be more substantial than those for ordinary walls. For a one-brick wall up to 1 m (3 ft 3 in) high, for example, use foundations 150 to 300 mm (6 to 12 in) deep and 375 to 450 mm (15 to 18 in) wide.

In some cases, the earth bank will have to be held back during the building process, to prevent it from collapsing onto the new brickwork. Formwork (see diagram) is ideal for this purpose, and can easily be made of timber struts and plywood. The formwork is placed against the face of the soil while you build. A gap of 300 to 600 mm (1 to 2 ft) should be left between the proposed wall and the formwork for easy movement while building.

When the lower courses are completed, mortar the drainage pipes in place so they extend into the hardcore – unless weepholes have been left. On long walls, be sure to add expansion joints at least every 10 m (33 ft) (see page 62). Once the wall is completed, leave the formwork for 24 hours to allow the mortar to dry before removing. Back-fill the trench behind the wall with hardcore and soil and compact well.

REINFORCING

Walls over 1 m (3 ft 3 in) high should be supported by end piers, as well as by intermediate piers, if they are quite long (see *Pillars and Piers*, page 34). Where piers are included in retaining brick walls, it is essential that they project from the face of the wall which is not in contact with the fill. They should also be bonded into the bonding system of the wall and must be the same height as the wall.

Under extreme pressure, bricks tend to buckle outwards. To prevent this, hooked metal rods can be set into the mortar joints of the wall, projecting through the back of the wall into retained earth where they are fixed to blocks of *in situ* concrete, acting as stabilizers.

Below: *Formwork in position.*

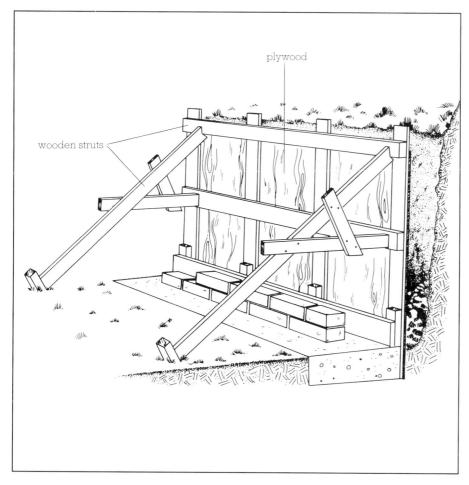

Step-by-step retaining wall

For a retaining wall, you need more substantial foundations, so roughly double the amounts of cement/sand/aggregate given for a one-brick wall on page 65.

Otherwise quantities are the same – but note that the bottom three courses of brick should be frost-resistant.

1 Peg out the area to be excavated and mark with string or a builder's line. Digging the soil out may be awkward because of the slope. You may also have to make use of formwork. Make sure the foundation depth is in keeping with the height of the wall as well as the weight which it will retain.
2 Lay your foundation (see Walls, page 63) and start laying bricks as soon as it is thoroughly dry. The number of weepholes required will depend on the size of the retaining wall. To accommodate a pipe you may have to chip off the corner of a brick. We used a PVC pipe, 40 mm (1½ in) in diameter.
3 Finish the wall off with paving bricks. Once all the bricks have been laid and the mortar has set, fill in the area between the earth and the wall with hardcore and soil. Even a low retaining wall will benefit from the extra drainage that hardcore provides.
4 A 50 mm (2 in) gap is wide enough to accommodate a drainage pipe. Hold it in place with mortar.

(diagram labels: plywood, wooden struts)

1

3

4

2

Walls

Wall finishes

If you can afford a good solid wall – and you can cut costs by building it yourself – make sure the finish will harmonize with the rest of your house and garden. Facing bricks should match other existing brickwork. For instance, a red brick wall should be avoided in a garden with autumn hued paving and it is usually best to give outdoor walls the same finish as the house.

Rendering (pargeting)

Render (parget) may be applied to many surfaces, including bricks and cement blocks. It may be put on smoothly for an even finish; applied in a rough manner to achieve a Spanish-style effect; or it may be stippled manually with a wet plaster mix in a simple stippling machine. Another alternative is to 'bag' the walls, by smearing on a wet plaster mix, so the profile of the bricks still shows.

Render requires the same ingredients as mortar (see page 87) for bricklaying. However, for an exterior wall which will be exposed to the weather, you will need to mix cement, lime and sand in the ratio of 1:1:6. For interior or protected patio walls, a weaker 1:2:9 mix may be used.

Apply the render with a plasterer's trowel, working from bottom to top and left to right (the other way around if you are left-handed). Once you have finished, splash some water onto the wall and trowel over the whole surface. When the render has hardened, continue trowelling it, using water every time, until you achieve a smooth finish.

Coping

Many free-standing walls benefit from a coping to give them an attractive finish and to throw the rainwater off. While tiles, slate, paving slabs or even wood may be used for coping, the usual practice with clay bricks is to use bricks on-edge or on-end, depending on the thickness of the wall. Paving bricks may also be used. Usually a plastered wall does not require a coping, but a combination can sometimes be effective: our step-by-step one-brick wall (see page 65) was rendered (pargeted), painted and then finished with facing bricks on-edge.

Manufacturers of concrete reconstituted stone walling also make single width and double width (overhanging) coping for use with their walling products to enable you to match and tone your colours exactly.

Right: *This brick wall has been finished off very effectively with curved clay coping bricks, which ensure that rainwater does not collect on the top of the wall.*

Above left: *Rendering (pargeting) can make an interesting contrast with the original brickwork. Brick pavers supply the finishing touch.*

Above: *A rendered (pargeted) and painted brick wall here provides an elegant setting for the inset planter.*

Right: *Sloped coping bricks and pier caps look very neat and shed rainwater most efficiently.*

Below: *On this curved wall, contrasting brick-on-edge coping cleverly frames the colourful flowers behind and looks very attractive.*

SCREEN BLOCK WALLS

Pierced screen concrete blocks can be used to provide a screen wall which allows air and light through – either on their own or combined with other walling materials. Each block may have its own pattern or it may take four blocks to make up the design. The block size is generally around 300 mm (12 in) square and the blocks are laid one on top of the other with no bonding pattern.

Proper support is essential for screen block walling. For vertical support, the blocks can be built between masonry block piers or you can use special matching grooved pilasters (into which the blocks fit) every 3 m (10 ft) or less. End pilasters have one groove, corner and intermediate pilasters have two and tee posts have three. For walls more than 1.2 m (4 ft) high, metal reinforcing rods (or lengths of angle iron) should be mortared into the (hollow) centre of the pilasters and reinforcing wire mesh incorporated into every other horizontal mortar joint.

A screen block wall can be built on top of a low masonry wall, or can be built on its own – either on top of paving slabs for a very low wall or with its own foundation similar to that used for a brick wall (see page 65) covered with an *in situ* concrete plinth. No part of the blocks should be below ground.

MATERIALS

To build a screen block wall, you will need normal bricklaying tools and a mortar mix of 1 part cement, 1 part plasticizer and 5 parts sand. Normal cement will tend to give a slightly dirty appearance to white concrete blocks so masonry cement could be used instead – or the mortar joints could be raked out afterwards and repointed with white mortar.

SETTING OUT

Exact measurement is essential when building a screen block wall as the blocks cannot be cut, so the overall wall length will need to be an exact multiple of the block size plus allowance for mortar and the pilasters.

Once the foundations have been laid, lay the bottom row of blocks and pilasters 'dry', allowing 10 mm or ⅜ in for each mortar joint so that you can mark out exactly where the wall will start and end, and where the pilasters will come. Note that the height of three pilasters usually equals two courses of block.

Above left: A screen block wall can provide a light and airy boundary.

Left: Screen blocks positioned on top of a low masonry wall.

Make up a gauge rod marked with the pilaster heights and the block heights.

Step-by-step screen block wall

For a wall 1.2 m (4 ft) high and 3 m (10 ft) long, you will need:

36 screen blocks
12 pilaster blocks
6 kg (13 lb) cement
30 kg or ¾ cu ft (66 lb) sand
6 kg (13 lb) lime
OR 12 ml (½ fl oz) plasticizer

Foundation
50 kg or 1 bag (110 lb) cement
145 kg or 3½ cu ft (320 lb) sand
235 kg or 5 cu ft (520 lb) aggregate

1 Prepare the foundation with a strip footing 300 mm (1 ft) wide with concrete at least 150 mm (6 in) deep. If reinforcing rods are being used, embed these in the concrete at the correct spacing. Build up from the footing either with a concrete plinth (built in formwork) or with a low masonry wall built between piers.

2 Build the first pier by placing an end pilaster on a mortar bed with the groove facing along the wall. Build up three pilaster blocks, checking that they are vertical and horizontal and using the gauge rod to ensure the correct height. Where reinforcing rods are used, pack the centre of each pier with mortar around the rod.

3 Position an intermediate pilaster block (or another end pilaster block for a short wall) the correct distance away and build this up in the same way. Position a string line across the blocks to mark the edges of the wall blocks.

4 Spread a 15 mm (⅝ in) layer of mortar on the foundations and inside the pilaster groove. Lay the first screen block in place, pressing it into the mortar.

5 Prepare a mortar bed on the foundation for the second block, but first 'butter' the side of the block to form the vertical joint.

6 With a spirit level and your gauge rod, check that the two blocks are level at the right height. If you need to tap a block down with a hammer handle, use a piece of wood to spread the load.

7 Work along the bottom course until you get to the position of the next pilaster pier and slot the last block into place. Build the second course of blocks in the same way and lay wire reinforcing strip along the whole wall from pier to pier. Then build up the piers by another three pilaster blocks and lay two more courses of blocks as before, placing the wire strip in the bottom mortar course. Do not attempt more than 1.2 m (4 ft) in the same day – let the mortar set first.

8 When you get to the required height, finish off the top with coping stones on the blocks and caps on the pilasters and, if necessary, point all the mortar joints.

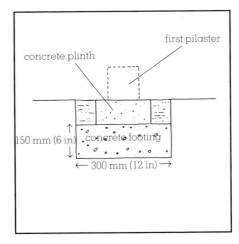

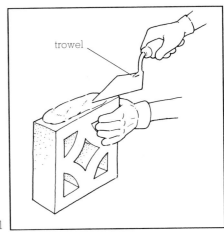

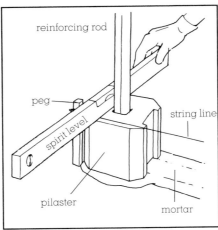

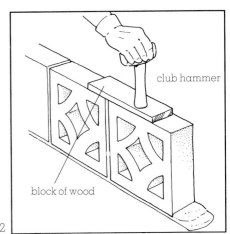

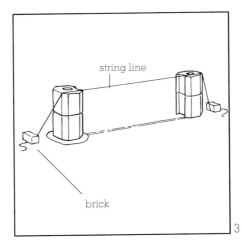

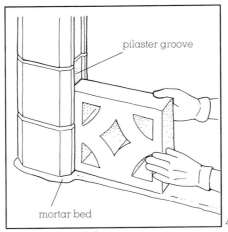

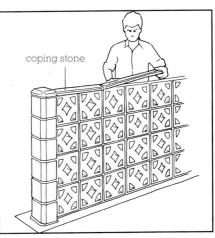

GARAGE

A GARAGE IS NOT ONLY SOMEWHERE TO KEEP THE CAR DRY AND SECURE, BUT IT IS ALSO USEFUL STORAGE SPACE FOR TOOLS AND MATERIALS. ERECTING A PRE-FABRICATED CONCRETE PANEL GARAGE IS A JOB WELL WITHIN THE CAPABILITIES OF THE AVERAGE HOMEOWNER, THOUGH IT IS A JOB WHICH IS BEST DONE WITH A HELPER.

Step-by-step garage

The first stage is to excavate the site and to lay a concrete base 100 mm (4 in) thick on a sub-base of 100 mm of hoggin (clayey gravel). This should be at least 100 mm (4 in) longer and 50 mm (2 in) wider than the garage, but check the detailed instructions with the garage. Lay the concrete slab level (i.e. with no drainage fall) and use a float to smooth a strip 300 mm (1 ft) wide around the edges.

Use general-purpose mix (1 part cement: 2 parts sand: 3 parts aggregate); for a slab of 20 sq m (215 sq ft), you will need 13 bags of cement, 1,350 kg (2,976 lb) of sand and 2,350 kg (5,181 lb) of aggregate. You will also need 3½ tonnes or 70 cu ft (3½ tons) of hoggin or a similar material. Allow the slab a week or so to cure before building the garage.

1 Mark out an exact right angle at one of the rear corners of the garage (using a

builder's square or the 3:4:5 method – *see page 84) and start in this corner bolting panels together. Ensure that each panel is vertical and that its external surface lines up with the previous panel and provide support until the whole back wall is built.*
2 To fit a window, use two short panels beneath the window opening, apply self-adhesive foam sealer around the window frame and then slot the window in place. A lintel is then bolted in place over the window.
3 The frame of a 'personal door' is secured to the adjacent panels with coach bolts and a lintel bolted in place above it. The door can be positioned either at the back of the garage or in one of the side walls.
4 Continue building the walls and then

Right: *The completed garage.*

3

4

5

start on the roof. A timber wall plate is fitted over the lintel at the front of the garage and timber 'firrings' (wall plates) along the side walls. Steel purlins are secured on top of the firrings to support the roof sheeting.

5 The link arm of the up-and-over (overhead) door is bolted to the front post of the garage.

6 The side tracks for the door are similarly bolted to the garage walls and the door can then be lifted into place and firmly secured in position, following the detailed fixing instructions supplied by the manufacturer with the garage equipment.

7 The final part of fitting the door is to fix the handle and the lock.

8 A general-purpose mastic sealant is used to seal all the joints outside the garage. Additional granules to match the finish of the garage are supplied which can be pushed into the surface of the mastic to camouflage the joints and give a uniform finish.

9 Inside, the joints should be pointed with a cement/sand mortar (1 part cement to 3 parts sand): the mortar should be rubbed into the joints by hand using an old glove and brushed down lightly before it has dried. Apply a cement mortar fillet where the garage walls meet the floor to ensure that there is no leakage and that the garage is watertight.

6

8

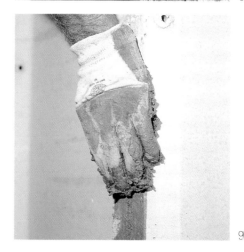

9

SMALL WEEKEND PROJECTS

THERE ARE LOTS OF SMALL PROJECTS DEMANDING MASONRY TECHNIQUES – MANY ARE SUITABLE FOR BEGINNERS WHO ARE NOT YET READY TO TACKLE LARGE AREAS OF PAVING OR A LONG WALL.

GARBAGE BIN SURROUND

Garbage bins can be an eyesore in the garden, but can easily be concealed by building a simple screen block wall three to five blocks high around it. This can also be used for trailing plants but will still allow light through. The walls can be built on their own foundations or on top of concrete paving slabs. You could also add a removable wooden roof, covered in roofing felt, to provide a setting for potted plants.

A more ambitious garbage bin surround could take the form of an L-shaped double wall with a planter in the middle – here constructed from random reconstituted stone.

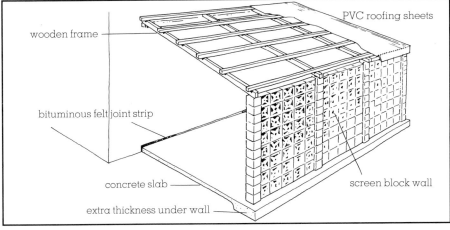

COMPOST BIN

Masonry can be used to construct a simple compost bin. A 100 mm (4 in) thick concrete slab forms the base; dense concrete blocks or bricks the walls. Leave weepholes to provide drainage and ventilation by excluding the mortar in some vertical joints in the bottom course of bricks. The finish on the concrete should be smooth for easy cleaning.

A compost bin should have at least two compartments and preferably three – one for two-year old compost ready to use, one for last year's compost (to use next year) and one for this year's fresh organic matter.

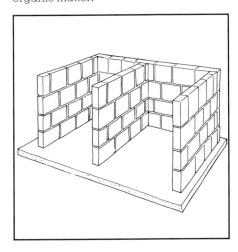

CARPORT

Screen block walling can be used to provide the support for a carport canopy. The ground slab needs to be 100 mm (4 in) thick concrete on top of 100 mm (4 in) of hoggin (clayey gravel) with the outer edge twice the thickness to act as a foundation for the wall. Use paving mix (1 part cement: 1½ parts sand: 2½ parts aggregate) and follow the instructions given on page 74 for building the screen block wall which must be reinforced with metal rods for added durability.

The roof structure can either be timber framing (as shown) or lightweight metal. Both should be covered with self-extinguishing sheeting (bitumen fibre sheeting). Follow the instructions.

SUNDIAL

A simple pillar, built from brick or concrete blocks, will provide the perfect setting for a sundial. This is an unusual feature which will provide a useful starting point for your building skills.

Detailed instructions on pillar building are given on page 37; if the sundial's own base is square, work out the positioning of the pillar, being careful to make sure that the sundial aligns when it is in the correct position relative to the sun. This is a handy way to tell the time when you are working outside!

Top and above: *Two types of garbage bin surround – one built using screen block walling and the other using reconstituted stone blocks.*

Above left: *Screen blocks with matching piers form this basic carport which has been roofed with corrugated PVC.*

Below left: *A useful compost area constructed using concrete blocks. Weepholes must be left in the bottom course to allow for drainage.*

Below: *An attractive plinth and pillar support for a sundial, built with matching bricks and pavers.*

Reference Information

CAREFUL PLANNING IS A VITAL PART OF SUCCESSFUL BRICKLAYING. BE SURE TO STUDY THE PRINCIPLES AND METHODS PROPERLY AND TO EQUIP YOURSELF WITH GOOD QUALITY TOOLS.

Tools and Materials

The basic toolkit required for outdoor brickwork projects (see illustration) is easily obtainable at all major do-it-yourself or hardware stores.

Tools

A straight-edge is made from a straight piece of wood, such as pine, and is used to level sand or concrete, or in conjunction with a spirit level.

A gauge rod is simply a flat, straightedged piece of wood which is marked off at intervals equal to one brick or block plus a mortar joint. It is used to ensure that masonry courses are kept regular. In addition, it can double as a straight-edge and may be used under a spirit level when the level is not long enough or to level sand or concrete.

Trowels are essential items for bricklaying. A large trowel is handy for spreading mortar, while a smaller trowel may be used as a pointing tool. A plasterer's float has a rectangular plate, used for spreading render on walls, and a corner trowel is shaped specifically to shape the mortar or render at corners.

Pointing tools are used to scrape out and shape the mortar joints in brickwork. A small pointing trowel, a special jointing tool or simply a piece of curved metal are all suitable, although each will create a different finish.

Corner blocks are used to string up builder's line as bricklaying progresses. They are not readily available commercially, but are easily and quickly made from wooden off-cuts (see page 86). Metal line pins may also be used.

A builder's square is used to check that corners are at right-angles. If a regular builder's square is not big enough, make one from three pieces of wood, cut in the ratio 3:4:5.

Brickwork Toolkit
1 straight-edge; 2 gauge rod; 3 plasterer's float; 4 corner trowel; 5 bricklaying trowel; 6 small pointing trowel; 7 jointer; 8 corner blocks; 9 builder's square; 10 mortar board; 11 rubber mallet; 12 two brick hammers; 13 bolster; 14 measuring tape; 15 chalk line reel/plumb bob; 16 ordinary plumb bobs; 17 tenon saw (backsaw); 18 scrubbing brush; 19 carpenter's pencil; 20 pegs; 21 builder's line; 22 two spirit levels.

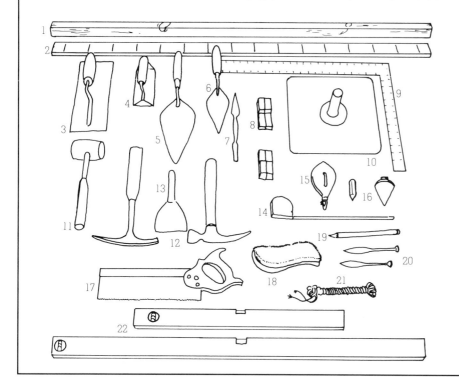

TOOLS AND MATERIALS

A mortar board is rather like a plasterer's hawk and is used to hold the mortar during work. Pieces of flat iron or drum tops make good substitutes for mortar boards.

A rubber mallet is used for tapping paving bricks, blocks or slabs into position. A wooden mallet could also be used or the wooden handle of a club hammer.

A brick hammer (or **ax**), which has a chisel end, is used for the rough cutting of bricks.

A brick bolster (**wide-bladed cold chisel** or **brick set**) has a spade-shaped chisel at one end and is used together with a club hammer (see page 90) to cut bricks.

A steel measuring tape is an indispensable item in the toolkit, used for measuring and checking distances, lengths and heights.

Plumb bobs come in various sizes, shapes and forms and are useful for checking that wall surfaces are vertical. The simplest plumb bob is attached to string and may be wound around a piece of wood to ensure it hangs securely. More expensive plumb bobs have a built-in line reel.

A tenon saw is useful for cutting the wood used to make a straight-edge, gauge rod or corner blocks.

A builder's line or **string** is used with either steel or wooden pegs to mark out an area where building or paving is to take place. It is also used to guide the level of each brick course during bricklaying.

Spirit levels are used to ensure that all surfaces are flat and level. They are available in several lengths with both a horizontal and vertical vial. Individual line levels are also available, working on the same principle as the spirit level, but serving specifically to check that a builder's line is level. The spirit level can double as a gauge rod, by marking off the courses on the underside.

In addition, you will need items such as spades, shovels, perhaps a pick, if excavating hard ground, a wheelbarrow and a scrubbing brush to clean mortar off paving. When long walls are built, a tingle must be used in combination with the corner blocks (see diagram on page 64) or line pins to support your string line. If a number of bricks need to be cut, it might be a good idea to hire an angle grinder or, for concrete paving blocks, a block splitter (masonry saw). Hire shops also supply plate vibrators (for laying concrete paving blocks) and hand compactors (for compacting hardcore or sand prior to laying paving or foundations).

MATERIALS

The basic ingredients of masonry work are bricks or concrete blocks, cement, sand and aggregate, as well as lime or plasticizer.

All of these are available from local suppliers. Pre-mixed quantities of sand, cement and aggregate – useful for small projects – are available from these same outlets in various-sized bags. Alternatively, check your local Yellow Pages for firms which will deliver materials in bulk.

For very large projects, such as laying a foundation slab for a garage or as a base for a drive or patio, *ready-mixed* concrete can be bought and delivered by truck. You must ensure that you have enough people to help unload it and spread it as soon as it arrives.

Bricks may be made from baked clay, cement or concrete and are available in a selection of shapes and sizes, at a variety of prices. The range includes ordinary bricks, facing bricks and thinner paving bricks – as well as highly durable engineering bricks. Your local supplier will be able to give you more information on the types of bricks available.

Although the proportions of ordinary clay bricks do vary a little, it is safe to assume that 60 bricks are required for one square metre (1.2 sq yd) of single walling.

Paving bricks are available in similar sizes to ordinary bricks, but are generally thinner. Remember that if you need accurate dimensions of bricks for planning (or other) purposes, it is wise to ascertain these by contacting the supplying manufacturer.

To achieve an exact match with existing brickwork, the use of second-hand bricks is often a good idea.

Concrete blocks also come in a range of shapes, sizes and finishes and in versions suitable for both paving and walling. Normal structural lightweight concrete blocks are not suitable for use in outdoor masonry (they have no aesthetic appeal and normally will be covered up in house building).

Concrete facing blocks for walling generally have one decorative face which will often include crushed stone aggregate to give a stone-like finish. Sizes can be regular or random – or they are available in large blocks which look like several smaller blocks already with mortar courses.

Cement may be bought in 50 kg or 100 lb bags from local supply stores. Most commonly used is ordinary Portland cement, which is suitable for both mortar and concrete work. White Portland cement is more expensive.

Cement bags should be closely stacked to a height of not more than 12 bags and they must be kept watertight. Ideally, store under cover, on waterproof plastic and covered with plastic, for not longer than two to three months.

If cement becomes lumpy due to damp, it should be used for unimportant work and then only if the lumps can be broken easily in one's hand.

Sand is the fine aggregate used for mixing mortar and concrete. Although it can be purchased in 50 kg or 100 lb bags from some suppliers, building sand is less expensive when ordered by the cubic metre (or cubic yard). It will be off-loaded in a pile outside your house. If you live in

a particularly windy area, make sure you cover it with plastic immediately.

Order 'soft' (bricklaying) sand for making mortar, and 'sharp' (concreting) sand for making concrete. Very fine 'silver' sand is used on concrete block paving after it has been laid, to fill in the gaps.

Aggregate (or ballast) is a mixture of coarser stones used for making concrete. It is available in 50 kg or 100 lb bags, or it may be ordered in bulk.

The important factor is the average size of the stones, which is why commercial suppliers ensure their aggregate is sieved prior to sale. It is available in several sizes. Note that the proportions given below are based on 20 mm (¾ in) aggregate, which is most commonly used for domestic work.

Sand and aggregate bought already mixed is often known as combined or 'all-in' aggregate.

Lime may be added to mortar to increase its binding and water-retentive properties. It is available in 25 kg or 50 lb sacks. Note that agricultural and road limes are not suitable for brickwork.

Plasticizer, available in minimum quantities of five litres (305 cu in), can be used instead of lime. For small projects where it would be wasteful to buy such a large quantity, it is quite acceptable to substitute the liquid soap, that is used for washing dishes.

Water is necessary to mix both mortar and concrete. Only ordinary tap water is suitable, sea water is not.

Reinforcing rods are necessary when building some pillars and piers. Made from metal, they are available from builders' merchants and supply stores.

Below: *A selection of masonry materials, including clay and concrete bricks, paving bricks and various facing bricks.*

BRICKWORK PRINCIPLES

Any experienced bricklayer knows that there are several golden rules when it comes to laying bricks. If your structure is not square, level and plumb, it simply will not have a professional finish and may not stand up properly.

Square

For a structure to be 'square', the sides making up its corners must be at a 90° angle to each other. For this reason, it is essential to check every corner with a builder's square as the wall (or other structure) takes shape. Never rely on guesswork or you will end up with crooked walls and uneven paving.

To set out a paved patio, or walls which meet at right angles, use the simple '3:4:5' method (see diagram). A corner formed in this way should always be exactly 90°. If in doubt, double-check the corner with your builder's square.

Level

It is essential to check your horizontal surfaces continually, including foundations and paving, with a spirit level. If a surface is not level it will slope, and a wall with sloping courses will immediately look peculiar – if, in fact, it stays up at all.

When the bubble is centred, you will know that the surface is level. If the spirit level is too short to use on large surfaces, put it on top of a longer straight-edge or straight length of wood.

Plumb

Applying a similar principle, a vertical surface which is not plumb will appear to lean. All vertical surfaces should therefore be checked continually.

When laying bricks, the simplest way of checking for plumb is to use your spirit level. On the other hand, a plumb bob may be used (see page 82) at corners and when setting up profiles, as well as for building garden walls.

It is not advisable to build when wet weather has been forecast, as heavy rain can wash freshly pointed mortar out of the joints. If this happens, the brickwork should be scrubbed clean as soon as possible to prevent staining. If necessary, use a proprietary masonry cleaning agent. Do not hose down newly pointed walls as the force of the water will have the same effect as heavy rain. If it does rain suddenly, drape plastic sheeting over brickwork to prevent any possible damage, securing the ends away from the brickwork with loose bricks.

Make certain that the brickwork will not receive any knocks before the mortar has hardened. If it is in a vulnerable position, erecting some type of barrier around the structure will help.

Never attempt to lay bricks in very cold weather – less than 3 °C or 37 °F. Remember that even in spring, clear sunny days often result in overnight frost which can damage uncovered work.

Setting out a square corner

Knock a peg into the ground at one corner of the site and measure and mark off 3 m (or 9 ft) to point A on a builder's line stretched along your base line, securing the line with a peg. Now fix a second line at the corner and mark a position 4 m (or 12 ft) at point B on this line and ask a helper to hold this tight at roughly 90° to the first line. With a second helper and a tape measure, adjust the angle of this second line until the distance between points A and B measures exactly 5 m (or 15 ft). The corner is now square and you can secure the line. Repeat for the three remaining corners and finally check that the diagonals are equal.

You can make a permanent builder's square with three pieces of wood nailed together such that the sides of the triangle formed are in the ratio 3:4:5 – say 0.9 m, 1.2 m and 1.5 m (or 3 ft, 4 ft and 5 ft).

Checking level A spirit level is essential for checking that all the horizontal surfaces are level.

Checking plumb A spirit level is also used to check vertical surfaces to ensure that they are plumb. As a final check, a plumb bob may also be used. This can be attached to a piece of wood so that it hangs clear of the brickwork surface.

See page 82 for details of these tools and how to use them.

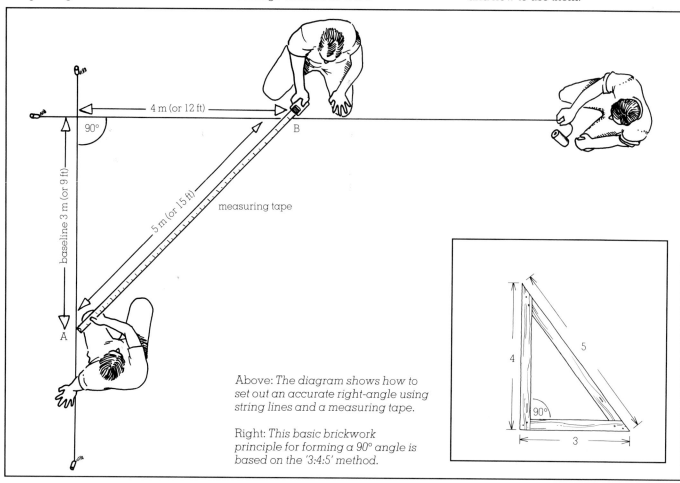

Above: *The diagram shows how to set out an accurate right-angle using string lines and a measuring tape.*

Right: *This basic brickwork principle for forming a 90° angle is based on the '3:4:5' method.*

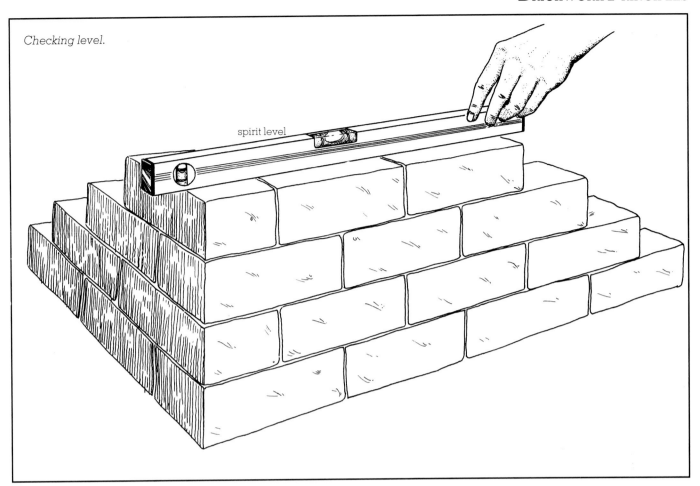

Checking level.

spirit level

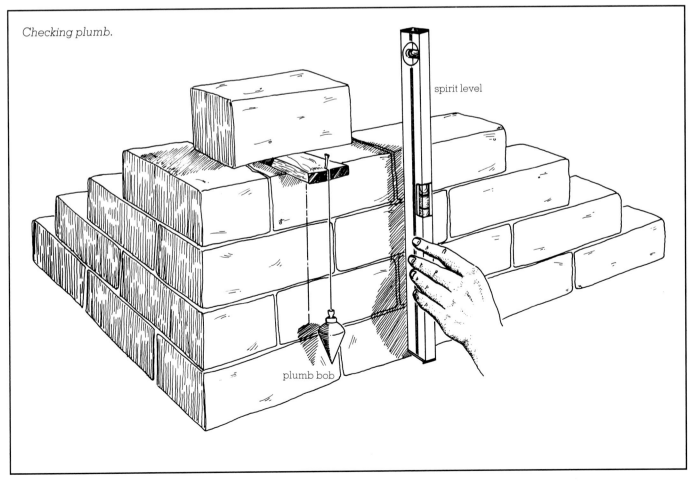

Checking plumb.

spirit level

plumb bob

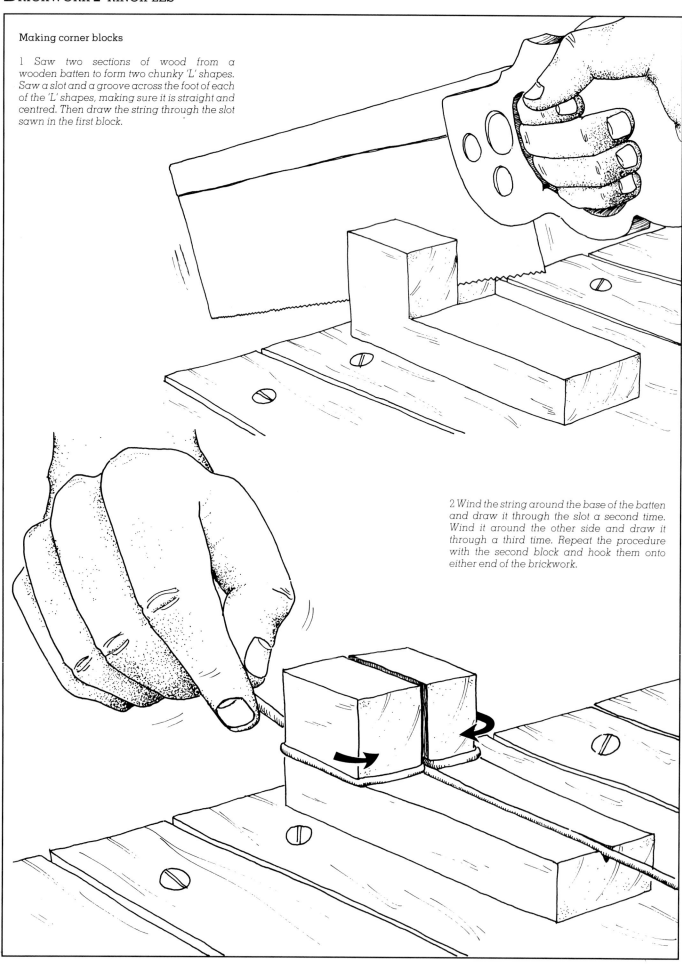

Making corner blocks

1 Saw two sections of wood from a wooden batten to form two chunky 'L' shapes. Saw a slot and a groove across the foot of each of the 'L' shapes, making sure it is straight and centred. Then draw the string through the slot sawn in the first block.

2 Wind the string around the base of the batten and draw it through the slot a second time. Wind it around the other side and draw it through a third time. Repeat the procedure with the second block and hook them onto either end of the brickwork.

QUANTIFYING MATERIALS

Before ordering materials you will have to assess your requirements. Base these on the following formulae and also use the quantities given with the various projects in this book as a guide.

Bricks are generally ordered in bulk. You will need 55–60 bricks for every square metre (1.2 sq yd) of single (sometimes called half-brick) walling. For every square metre (1.2 sq yd) of paving, you will need about 45 bricks.

Concrete is a mixture of sand, cement, aggregate and water. It is used for foundations, for walls or as a slab for buildings and paved areas in other materials. It can also be used on its own as a paving material. The thickness and proportions required will depend on the kind of brickwork you plan to undertake. The recommended depths of foundations are detailed for the various projects in this book. To ascertain the volume of concrete needed, simply multiply the length x width x depth of the foundation.

Use the following recommendations to ascertain the ratio of materials required. General purpose mix is suitable for most uses, except foundations and exposed paving. Cement, sand and 20 mm (¾ in) aggregate are mixed in the proportions 1:2:3 (1:4 if you are using a combined aggregate). Foundation mix is used for footings, foundations and bases for pre-cast paving. Mix cement, sand and aggregate in the proportions 1:2½:3½ (1:5 for combined aggregate). Paving mix is suitable for all exposed paving, especially drives. Mix cement, sand and aggregate in the proportions 1:1½:2½ (1:3½ for combined aggregate) – or use ready-mixed concrete.

Mortar, the general name for any mixture of cement, sand and water, is used for bedding and jointing brickwork. It is also used in the form of render (parget) to cover walls if required. Mortar mixes vary according to the type of work being done and the strength of mortar required.

A mix of 1 part cement to 1 part builder's lime and 5 to 6 parts sand is suitable for exterior brickwork. One bag (50 kg or 110 lb) of cement mixed as above will lay approximately 600 bricks. For retaining or exposed walls, use a stronger mix: 1 part cement, ½ part lime and 4 parts sand (400–500 bricks/50 kg bag). Plasticizer can be used instead of lime.

Plasticizer Use about 50 ml with every 50 kg of cement (1½ fl oz with 100 lb), in place of lime. For small projects, use the equivalent quantity of liquid soap.

Render requires the same ingredients as mortar used for bricklaying and bedding. For a wall which will be exposed to the weather, you will need to mix cement, lime and sand in the ratio of 1:1:6. For interior or protected patio walls, the proportions of lime and sand may be increased to 1:2:9.

Integral water-proofing solution is available in handy sized packs (2½ litres). Add 1 litre per 50 kg (110 lb) of cement for water-proofing against ground water pressure and ½ litre per 50 kg (110 lb) for general rendering and concrete work.

Mixing materials

The technique used for mixing both concrete and mortar is exactly the same.

First, thoroughly mix the dry materials on a hard, clean, dry and level surface. Then form a crater in the centre and gradually add enough water to make the mixture pliable. When adding the last of the water, be careful, as it tends to become too wet very suddenly.

Carefully mix from the outside inwards, preventing the water from escaping. Too little water will make the mixture stiff, porous and difficult to work with, while too much will weaken it and cause the cement to 'float'. The consistency of concrete should be soft, rather like thin porridge. Mortar must be workable and spread easily.

Consider the weather when mixing materials. Frost may mean that you have to postpone mixing your concrete, and rain could affect your mix dramatically.

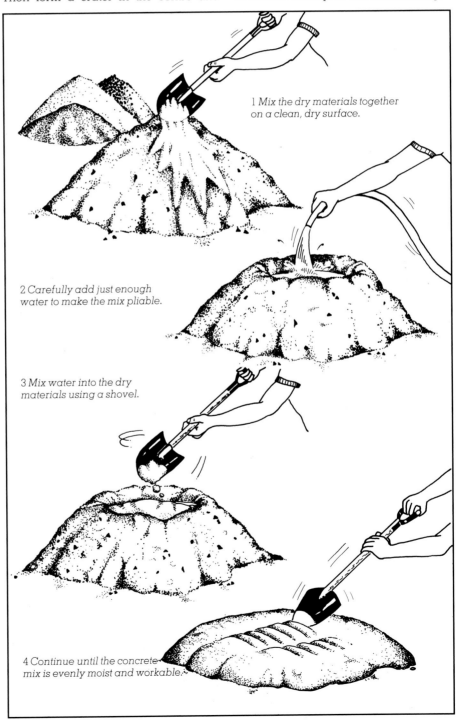

1 *Mix the dry materials together on a clean, dry surface.*

2 *Carefully add just enough water to make the mix pliable.*

3 *Mix water into the dry materials using a shovel.*

4 *Continue until the concrete mix is evenly moist and workable.*

SETTING OUT SLOPES

Patios, driveways and paths must have a slight slope away from the house or any other building so that water cannot accumulate and undermine the foundations. This gradient may not be evident to the naked eye, since a mere 10 mm for every 1 m (½ in/4 ft) or a gradient of 1-in-100, is adequate along a path or drive, though paths and driveways should incorporate a fall of 1 in 40 in a consistent direction across their width, as well as their length. For patios or paving by the house a slope of 1 in 50 is generally recommended.

There are several ways of measuring a drainage slope, the most usual being to use a spirit level on a straight-edge with a block underneath one end. Read the spirit level in the normal way (with the bubble centred). The size of the wooden block used will depend on the length of your straight-edge and the slope required – for a 1 in 50 slope, for example, a piece of wood 40 mm thick is suitable for a straight-edge 2 m long (or 1 ½ in for a 5 ft straight-edge). This will enable you to establish the correct slope easily and to keep it consistent, so that you can set up your building line along it.

A rubber or plastic hose can also be used to determine a slope (as well as to check levels). This method, which is based on the principle that water finds its own level, is especially useful over a long gradient or around a corner.

To measure a fall of, say, 25 mm in 3 m (1 in/10 ft) take two wooden stakes, each about 750 mm (2 ft 6 in) long. Mark off 500 mm (20 in) from the top of one stake and 525 mm (21 in) on the other. Set them into the ground, 3 m (10 ft) apart, knocking in the first stake to the 500 mm (20 in) mark. Now set two short pieces of transparent plastic tubing (obtainable from some motor spares shops) into either end of the hose.

Attach one end of the hose to the first stake with wire, so that the tubing is opposite the top of the stake. (Note that the hose may be any length for this method to work, which means that you do not have to cut up your hose in order to make it fit.) Fill the hose with water until the water in the tubing is level with the top of the first stake.

Hold the other end of the hose in position next to the second stake, and, with the hose held against the stake, knock the stake into the ground, until the top is at the same level as the water in the transparent tubing. Check back at the first stake and add more water if necessary to reach the required height. Now attach the hose to the stake with wire.

Mark two points 450 mm (18 in) from the top of the first stake and 475 mm (19 in) from the top of the second stake and tie a builder's line between them. This now gives you a guide for excavating to the correct slope until you get down to the two original marks.

Two Methods of Setting out a Slope

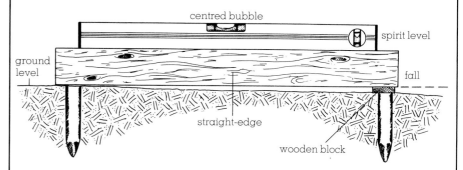

Above: *Place a block of wood under one side of the straight-edge, to allow for the required slope, before taking a regular spirit level reading.*

Below: *Utilizing the principle that water finds its own level, a hose is used to set out a slope of 25 mm/3 m (1 in/10 ft) – see text for details.*

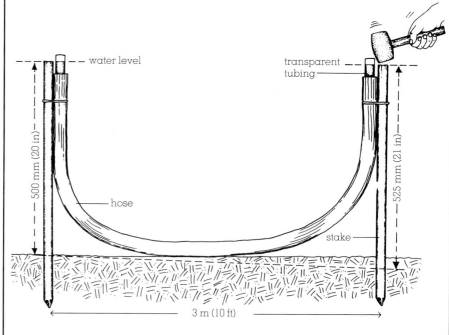

Marking out a Circle

Below: *Knock a peg into the ground at a central point; attach a piece of string with a stick fixed to the other end; pull* the string taut across the radius and then mark the circle in the ground with the stick.

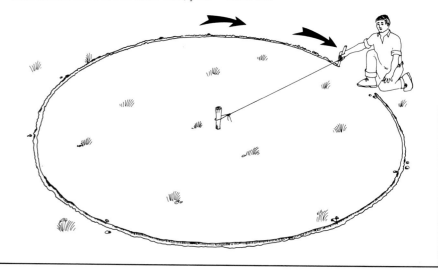

Bricklaying Techniques

Before attempting to lay bricks, it is important to practise using a trowel, as you will need it to form a bed of mortar for your first, most important course and thereafter to spread and butter the bricks with mortar as the wall takes shape.

Bedding bricks in mortar is what bricklaying is all about. Once your concrete foundation is thoroughly dry, set out your first course of bricks without mortar, to ensure they fit. Mix your mortar, in manageable amounts, on a firm, dry surface and pick up a small amount by pushing your trowel sideways into the mixture, then lifting it. Lay a sausage-shaped bed of mortar, 10 to 12 mm (approximately ½ in) thick and 100 mm (4 in) wide, along the line where your first course of bricks will be laid. To ensure that all your walls will be straight, you need to lay a builder's square along the slightly flattened lines of mortar. With the point of a trowel, draw a straight line in the mortar to indicate where the outer edge of the bricks will be. Remove the square and run a furrow down the centre of the mortar to allow better bonding with the first course of bricks.

You can either butter the ends as you work (see below), or fill in the gaps between the bricks once they have been laid. Lay the first brick, using the line and the furrow in the mortar as a guide. Follow the pattern shown when the bricks were laid without mortar and lay the first course of bricks. Continue to spread mortar on each subsequent course, scraping excess mortar off the sides of the brickwork as you press and tap each one into place until it is level.

Set up corner blocks or line pins with a builder's line to help maintain a straight edge. Each corner brick or block must be checked for height with the gauge rod. The vertical and horizontal levels are then checked with the spirit level, adding (or removing) mortar from under the bricks if necessary. Use a builder's square to double check that all corners are at right angles. These safeguards will ensure that you do not end up with lopsided walls. If you find that any bricks are lying skew, tap them gently into place with the handle of your bricklaying trowel. Fill any gaps between bricks with mortar before you lay the second course of bricks.

Using your spirit level and gauge rod, check your levels and planes continually. This is essential because any discrepancies will soon become obvious and may also make your brickwork unstable and thus dangerous.

Check all surfaces throughout to ensure vertical walls. If your corners are skew, the entire structure will be out of alignment. Place the spirit level diagonally against the bricks as well as in a horizontal and vertical position.

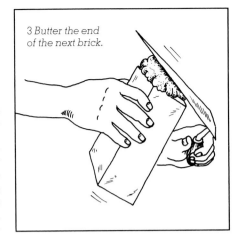
3 Butter the end of the next brick.

4 Slide the brick into position.

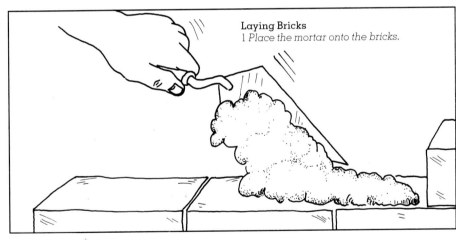
Laying Bricks
1 Place the mortar onto the bricks.

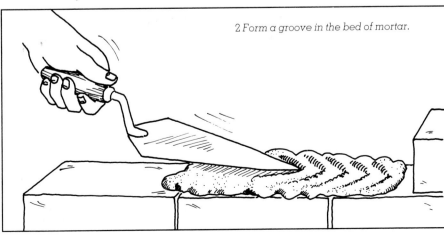
2 Form a groove in the bed of mortar.

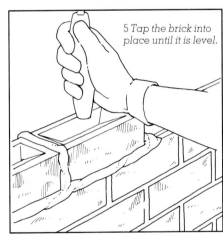
5 Tap the brick into place until it is level.

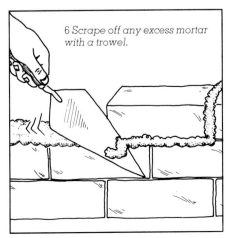
6 Scrape off any excess mortar with a trowel.

Bricklaying Techniques

Buttering bricks is an art which must be mastered before any large-scale bricklaying can be done. To do this, lift a small amount of mortar with the trowel and spread it onto the end of the brick to be laid. Squash the mortar down firmly to ensure it does not drop off and then lay the brick in place.

Cutting bricks manually is relatively simple once you acquire the knack. This can be done with a brick hammer (ax) or with a bolster (wide-bladed cold chisel or brick set) and a club hammer. To cut a brick with a brick hammer (ax), hold the brick in your hand and, using the chisel end, tap a line all around the brick where you want it to break. A final, sharp blow on this cutting line should result in its breaking evenly along the line.

To use a bolster, place the brick on the ground (ideally on a bed of sand) and score the surface on all sides with the chisel end. Then hold the bolster firmly on the cutting line and gently tap the handle several times with the club hammer. Once again, a final, sharp blow should result in its breaking neatly in two.

Right: *Cutting a brick with a bolster (chisel) and a club hammer.*

Below: *Cutting a brick with the chisel end of a brick hammer (ax).*

Working with Concrete

The basic ingredients of concrete are cement, sand and aggregate – see page 87 for details of the different mixes.

When the dry ingredients of concrete are mixed with water, a reaction starts, causing the cement particles to stick to one another, to the sand and aggregate particles and to anything else such as surrounding brick – and even metal (including your concreting tools if you do not clean them!).

Concrete takes some time to set once it has been mixed. Unless retardants have been used, it remains 'workable' for between 1½ and 2 hours but it takes three days before it has any useful strength. After seven days, concrete will have two-thirds of its ultimate strength – it is then important to prevent it from drying out. This can be done by covering it with polythene or damp sacking and, if it is very dry, by spraying it with water – the hardening process is one of curing rather than one of drying out.

Laying concrete

Details of mixing, site preparation and foundations are covered elsewhere in this book. Here, we look at the actual process of laying the concrete once it is mixed and ready to use.

Except where concrete is being poured into a prepared trench, formwork is essential to hold it in place while it cures. Normally, this will be lengths of wood securely held in place and with no gaps at the corners or the edges through which stray concrete could escape. Formwork can either be wood (at least 25 mm or 1 in thick) held in place with pegs firmly driven into the ground, or special steel 'roadforms' – these are particularly useful for making curved areas.

Concrete is placed on the prepared site by upending a wheelbarrow (taking care not to damage the sides of a trench or the formwork) or from the chute leading to a ready-mix delivery truck. Shovels are used to spread it evenly over the site allowing a little for compaction.

Compaction itself can be carried out either with a hand compactor (suitable for stiffer concrete used in trenches) or with a tamping beam – a length of 50 x 150 mm (2 by 6 in) wood held on edge. This is used in a sawing motion across the area – not simply dragged along the tops of the side forms. If the concrete still shows an open texture, it is undercompacted and more concrete should be shovelled on and the process repeated.

Concrete finishes

Concrete can be finished in several different ways.

If left as tamped, it will have a level but rippled finish – depending on how well the tamping was carried out. If the leading edge of the tamping beam is slightly raised during the final tamping, a slightly rippled but otherwise smooth struck-off

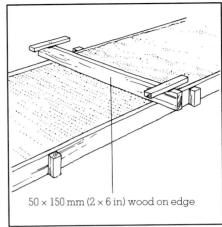

50 × 150 mm (2 × 6 in) wood on edge

Above left and right: Compaction can either be carried out with a hand compactor or with a tamping beam – a straight length of wood.

finish will be produced on the concrete.

A soft broom can be used to give a fairly smooth finish while a stiff nylon broom will give a pronounced 'corduroy' texture, which is especially suitable for paths and drives.

An exposed aggregate finish can be produced by spreading loose coarse aggregate on the fresh concrete after initial tamping and then tamping this firmly in with a float. When the concrete has hardened a little, brush and spray the surface with water which leaves the aggregate exposed, highlighting its colour and texture. Finish off with a stiff broom 24 hours later.

A fine sandpaper-like finish can be produced on concrete by using a wooden float on the surface before it has gone off, while a steel float, if kept clean, will give a very smooth finish.

Below: Various finished surface effects can be produced on concrete. Decide whether you wish to have a smooth or rough look and you can then choose your method accordingly.

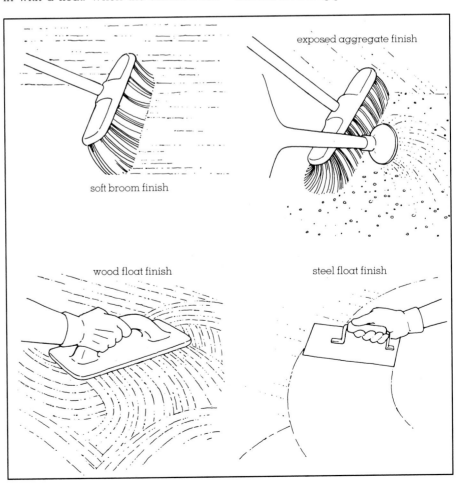

exposed aggregate finish

soft broom finish

wood float finish

steel float finish

Step-by-step concrete slab

The concrete slab and surround foundation shown here were the basis for a paving slab patio and concrete brick wall surround. Because the ground was soft, concrete foundations were used and, because a large quantity was needed, we used ready-mixed concrete (Mix C7.5P to BS5238, high workability, 20 mm maximum aggregate).

The patio measured 4.05 m (13 ft 4 in) × 2.25 m (7 ft 5 in) and a 600 mm (2 ft) wide foundation was used for the walls. 50 mm (2 in) of hardcore was used for both the foundation and the patio sub-base and 50 mm (2 in) of fine concreting sand for the patio. The materials you will need to construct this concrete slab are:

Patio sub-base
790 kg or 15.8 cu ft (1738 lb) hardcore
632 kg or 15.8 cu ft (1390 lb) fine concreting sand
0.68 cu m (24 cu ft) ready-mixed concrete

Wall foundation
510 kg or 10.2 cu ft (1122 lb) hardcore
0.87 cu m (30.7 cu ft) ready-mixed concrete

1 The prepared site showing turf and topsoil removed and trenches dug for the foundation with depth pegs in place around the edge of the patio area.
2 Formwork erected around the slab, hardcore put in place and well-compacted and the patio surface 'blinded' with sand which is then rolled out level.
3 Help is at hand for shovelling the ready-mixed concrete directly from the delivery lorry into the foundation trenches up to the level of the pegs. It is important to work quickly at this point before the concrete sets or the weather conditions change.
4 More ready-mixed concrete is shovelled into the patio area and levelled off with a tamping beam using the formwork as a guide.
5 The formwork is left in place until the compacted concrete sets hard. It can then be removed altogether.

4

5

Useful Addresses

United Kingdom

Service	Organisation	Telephone	Nature of Service
Architects and Surveyors	Faculty of Architects & Surveyors 15 St Mary Street Chippenham, Wilts SN15 3JN	0249 655398	Lists of members
	Incorporated Association of Architects & Surveyors Jubilee House, Billing Brook Road Weston Favell, Northants NN3 4NW	0604 404121	Lists of members
	Royal Institute of British Architects (Clients Advisory Service) 66 Portland Place London W1N 4AD	071 580 5533	Lists of members, plus standard forms of contract
	Royal Institution of Chartered Surveyors 12 Great George Street London SW1P 3AD	071 222 7000	Lists of members
Builders	Building Employers Confederation 82 New Cavendish Street London W1M 8AD	071 580 5588	Lists of BEC-registered builders
	Federation of Master Builders 33 St John Street London WC1N 2BB	071 242 7583	Lists of members
Building Materials	Asphalt & Coated Macadam Association 25 Lower Belgrave Street London SW1 0LS	071 730 0761	Advice on specifications
	British Aggregate Construction Materials Industries 156 Buckingham Palace Road London SW1W 9TR	071 730 8194	Lists of members supplying materials and laying drives
	Brick Development Association Woodside House, Winkfield Windsor, Berks SL4 2DX	0344 885651	Technical advice on using bricks, plus useful literature
	Building Centre Group 26 Store Street London WC1E 7BT Also in Bristol, Glasgow and Manchester	071 637 1022 (technical) 0344 884999 (literature)	Displays of building products and equipment, manufacturers' literature, bookshop
	Cement & Concrete Association Wexham Springs, Slough Berks SL3 6PL	02816 2727	Technical advice plus useful literature

Australia and New Zealand

Service	Organisation*	Nature of service
Architects and Surveyors	Royal Australian Institute of Architects	List of members, advisory service, contract forms
	New Zealand Institute of Architects	List of members, advisory service, contract forms
	Surveyors' Board	List of approved practitioners
Builders	Builders Licensing or Registration Board	List of licensed builders and sub-contractors
	Housing Industry Association	List of members (builders and sub-contractors), advisory service
	Master Builders Association	List of members, contract forms, dispute arbitration
Building materials	Australian Asphalt Pavement Association	Advisory service, list of members
	Brick Development and Research Institute	Technical publications and advice
	Building Information Centres	Materials display, manufacturers' literature
	Cement and Concrete Association of Australia	Advisory service, technical library
	Concrete Masonry Association of Australia	Technical advice and literature
	New Zealand Concrete Masonry Association	Technical advice and literature
	New Zealand Portland Cement Association	Advisory service, technical publications and library
	New Zealand Standards Association	Standards for materials and constructional techniques
	Standards Association of Australia	Standards for materials and constructional techniques

*Please see your local telephone directory for the addresses and telephone numbers of offices in each state.

INDEX